There's More to Life than the Pursuit of Money

Glen Coffee Sr. & Glen Coffee Jr.

ISBN 978-1-64191-358-4 (paperback)
ISBN 978-1-64191-428-4 (hardcover)
ISBN 978-1-64191-359-1 (digital)

Christian Faith Publishing, Inc.
832 Park Avenue
Meadville, PA 16335
www.christianfaithpublishing.com

Printed in the United States of America

Acknowledgments

The relentless pursuit of following Jesus, is a quest that God never intended for us to do alone. Some of the same people that are taking this splendid journey, are the ones we want to thank for helping us with our book:

To our Lord and Savior Jesus Christ- Glen and I totally understand that "There's more to life than the pursuit of Money" is an assignment from God! And that this precious message will be a movement for His people. We are so thankful for this amazing task!

To Glen Jr., my son- I love your humble character. When you retired from the San Francisco 49ers and so "eloquently" told the world, "There's more to life than the pursuit of Money!" That gave me a re-newed spirit and I will always love you for that! You are the coolest, the smoothest, most God-fearing person that I know.

To my beloved children Maneche, Rosh, Leah and Matthew. Also, my two beautiful granddaughters Xyla and Ava. Thank you all for your continued love and support!

To my mom, Miss Abbie Coffee- Thank you for being a praying mother and a great provider. Most importantly, thank you for teaching me that "fear" is not an option in my life!

To my brother, CEO & Founder@INFO@PETADERM.COM, Mr. Kendy Coffee- Thank you for being a Godly man and providing a refuge and a safe haven for me to finish my portion of our book!

To the University of Alabama- We are so thankful to Coach Nick Saban, Coach Burton Burns, the faculty, Alumni and all the fans for molding Glen Jr. into the awesome man he is today! ROLLTIDE

To Coach Mike Singletary and the San Francisco 494ers- Thank you for giving Glen Jr. the opportunity to play in the National Football League! Most importantly, thank you for supporting Glen's decision to pursue his ministry!

To our publicist, Rebecca Minder- Glen and I are so thankful that you are so committed to our book. We know in our hearts, without a doubt that God sent you to us to ensure that this profound message goes global! ROLLTIDE

To Charlotte Milner- Thank you for being a close friend and creating an incredible network for Glen and me. We are honored to be members of the Bamasanantonio Alumni chapter! ROLLTIDE

To Don Butler- God spoke to me through you at just the right time in my life. Thank you for encouraging Glen Jr. and I to writing our profound book!

To the United States Armed Forces- Glen and I are so thankful that we had the honor and privilege to fight for and defend the greatest nation in the world! GOD BLESS AMERICA!!!

Glen Coffee Sr.

Foreword

Apologies...

I wonder if I've been a quitter all of my life. Middle school football first comes to mind. Full of confidence and self-determination, I strutted out of my coach's office proud in accomplishment. What was accomplished, you ask? The leaving behind of my second love (Nintendo came first) and the beginning pursuit of NBA dreams. You see, I was good at football, really good, but it left me internally stressed. I always worried about being the best, looking the best or questioning did I do enough. Prior to 7th grade, basketball barely registered within my conscious. Dribbling a basketball without looking un-athletic and possessing a mean first step was the extent of my basketball expertise. For reasons long forgotten, my P.E. ritual switched from doing "whatever," to running up and down the courts. It was freeing in a way I'd never previously experienced with any sport. All of a sudden football seemed so regimented, almost controlling. Basketball allowed me to channel my inner MJ and dominate every aspect of the game. Often I'd leave the court leading in assists, points, rebounds, blocks, everything. Keep in mind, of course, we're talking, athletically speaking, less-than-challenging opposition. The guys on the actual b-ball team rarely graced those P.E. courts with their presence. In my head, however, it didn't matter, the sport felt natural and, with hard work, I intended to make it a career. Confident in my first step off the dribble, I quit football.

Could I have done both? Of course, but that meant even less time for gaming, so that was that.

"I" quit football, Doris Coffee on the other hand, hadn't. Little did young Glen Coffee know that Coach Vincent had already relayed the message to his mother, an un-consulted and unsuspecting mother. It was a bold move not to tell her and in witnessing her get out of the car, the realization hit, it was a stupid move. Without a word she promptly, as it is in the movies, grabbed my ear and walked me back into coach's office. Football it is. From that point on my conscience began to question every norm of society. Was what the majority considered good, bad and okay, truly good, bad and okay? Such questioning led me down endless confusing thought processes. Confusing because instead of working toward being an individual, being myself, I sought to be "normal." Not only normal but seeking to meet other people's expectations while being ignorant to the fact that I was able to let my own expectations for myself weigh in on the matter. For instance, why is it expected that I play football just because I'm athletic and good at it? Maybe in truth my time could be spent in the pursuit of something else. At that age however, I couldn't fathom alternative possibilities. Lost to me was what that "something else" looked like (take school seriously maybe?). This in turn led to inner turmoil, which developed into a self-indulging attitude of, "as long as it doesn't hurt anybody, I'm going to do what I want." Problem is, in looking back, I've hurt plenty. My child, her mother, my friends, family, etc. You see, we were created first, for the Creator, then for each other. Matthew 22:36-40.

If I get paid to play football, then maybe I'll tolerate it. That was the thought that led me to forgo my final season at The University of Alabama. Living up to other people's expectations still held sway over my actions. Now, however, I felt encouraged to stir the pot. To do what I wanted to do while still satisfying the masses. Would

I have stayed my senior year of college knowing what I know now? Without a doubt. Would I do it over again if I could? No way. Our mishaps are God's ice cream. He salivates at the opportunity to pick us up after a fall or redirect us when we ignore the Holy Spirit. Let's fast forward to the San Francisco 49ers. Up to this point I had found Christ, helped bring a child into the world, and found myself with a lot of money. All three would become tools that I used to not only justify my depressed state but also blame football for what I felt. To justify selfish wants, desires, and lust. To justify retiring from the NFL or, better yet, quitting the NFL. You see, along with my contract, I had broken my word to the 49er organization. Unfortunately in my head, egotistical feelings and emotions had masked themselves under the label, "rightful yearnings of a righteous man." And so to anybody involved with that team, past, present, and future…I'm sorry.

Have you ever wondered what the military is like? In asking anyone who's ever served, assuming they go into any detail, they will have an answer as ambiguous as life itself. One thing I can say with near certainty is that the progression of "self" is comparable to, if not surpassing, the growth of one's self that occurs with the combined years of high school and college. My core beliefs and habits didn't change much within those schooling years. I knew better concerning this or that after the revelation of Jesus Christ in my life, but little changed. Being what I thought was a good person was still good enough for me. Military service taught me the need of others, the importance of relationship. My military career began with me in pursuit of the "green beret." Green Berets are technically speaking the US Army Special Forces. People use the term "special forces" for other specialized units but the correct term for these units--i.e., Navy Seals and Army Rangers--is special operations or special operation forces. Again I found myself at a crossroads, except this time, my daughter instead of faith was the vehicle that I used to again make everything about me. Maybe a year-and-a-half of service had gone by and I still couldn't cope with fact that I ended my relationship with my child's mother. Cope with the fact that I somehow was fine with my little girl being raised under another man's roof. Cope with the fact that I told God, "My family isn't good enough." I again gave up.

It was 5:00 a.m., my fellow Special Forces candidates were gearing up for what was to be our second-to-last field training exercise. Ten days of this particular training mission and a month of the one to follow and I'd be on the home stretch. Literally. Upon graduation of the course, I would have been sent to 7th Group, which was housed ten minutes outside of my hometown. Unfortunately, 5:00 a.m. witnessed me walking up to formation nearly drunk, rather, fairly tipsy. Not only intoxicated, but carrying one of the wine bottles that helped me get to my current state. What a spectacle that must have been. I didn't have the courage, if I can call it such, to simply say, "I know longer want to continue in this course." What resulted was myself getting dropped from the Q (qualification) course. After being held in a holding unit for about five months, I ended up being home anyway, stationed at Camp Rudder. It's a base that helps facilitate the training of Ranger School. Hence, the media and many people thinking I was and am an Army Ranger. I simply drove boats on a river in a safety observance role. You would think my self-pity had run its course considering my daughter now lived ten minutes away. Yet, being around life-long friends gave me the excuse I needed to be out four nights a week. Those nights of guilt led to the eventuality of a failed drug test and an accompanying General (Under Honorable Conditions) chaptering out of the Army. "General under honorable conditions" … at least it sounds polite. So again, I apologize. To the military, SF Cadre, and anyone I served with, I'm sorry.

Unfortunately it doesn't stop there. Soon after my father began to write this story, I pitched him an idea. The plan was for him to write his part with little help from me while I simultaneously wrote my part, paralleling his chapters in the process. See kind of how I was thinking? You'd have insight into a father's perspective along with his son's "this is what actually went down" narrative. As you'll find out, he got two chapters out of me. Looking back, I realize that I was scared to write, scared to reveal the truth. What an opportunity it would have been to show how the Lord strengthened me every time I allowed weakness to overtake me. As you read this book, just know the light my father sees in me is real, true, and right. This is due in no small part to the willfully ignorant choices I've touched on in this section of the book. Everything we do, even what we consider "bad," is for the good of His glory. "And we know that ALL things work together for the good to them that love God, to them who are called according to his purpose," Romans 8:28. So I say to you as well, Pop, Sorry. Sorry for allowing fear to paralyze me.

And to my mother. You have had the biggest role of anybody in my life. You instilled in me a foundation on which to build a house. That house hasn't yet been built but believe me, Mom, it's coming. I'm not going to tell you "sorry" because I can hear the scoff you'd make if I did. I can now see that this is what makes moms so special, so strong. Y'all were built to handle taking on the burdens and mishaps of families without hearing "thank you" and "sorry." I must, however, thank you, and instead of sorry, "my bad." I just pray that any embarrassment or anything you may have felt, made you stronger. In fact, I know it has. Not once did you wavier in your affection or doubt of what I can accomplish. I love you, Mom, and get ready. I'm not finished.

Glen Coffee Jr.

Introduction

On a Thursday evening practice at the San Francisco 49er's practice field, a second-year running back from the University of Alabama left abruptly with no explanation. On Friday afternoon the second-year back shockingly announced his retirement from the NFL after just playing one year in the league.

Proud to say, this player's name is Glenwood Razeem Coffee Jr., my son! Glen announced his retirement August 13, 2010, and I didn't even know it! I was working for the Emerald Coast YMCA in Fort Walton Beach, Florida, at the time. While at work, one of my lawyer friends called me and said, "Glen, I'm watching CNN, and your son just announced his retirement from the 49ers!"

Of course, my heart sank and I was very concerned. But I told my friend that as soon as I got off the phone with him that I was going to call Glen and get on the top of this situation, giving him the impression that I was going to fix everything!

I would soon discover that it was nothing for me to fix and that Glen had made the right decision by submitting to God's authority!

I immediately called Glen, and he was still in the press conference. We briefly talked, but it seemed like a lifetime. I just wanted to make sure that he was okay, and I asked him, "Son, are you all right?"

He responded, "Yes, Dad, I'm good."

Of course, I asked him, "Why did you retire?"

He said, "Dad, I can't talk long, but I will call you back. But I was in the practice field locker room, and God came to me and start talking to my heart! He said, 'Glen, I want you to retire from the NFL and go out into the world and spread my word!'"

Glen told me that he tried to rationalize with God by saying, "All my life I have wanted to be a professional football player, and you want me to give this life up. I CAN'T DO THAT, GOD!"

Glen told me that after he tried to negotiate with God, He came at him straight up and told him, "If you say that you love me, then give up football, all of it. I AM GOD!"

Then Glen told me that he submitted to God and told Him, "Okay, here I am. I'm yours!"

As Glen's story started to unfold, the Holy Spirit came to me and God started talking to me as well unexpectedly! As I stated I was at work. I didn't want to, but I started crying at work in front of all my coworkers. It was embarrassing at first, but then I didn't care because the Almighty God noticed me of all people and had a message for me!

I wasn't just weeping, I was crying, crying like the tears would not stop flowing and the snot from my nose just kept coming!

At first I felt important, chosen, blessed because the Almighty God had noticed me, a speck of sand on the beach, then I trembled because I realized that God, being God, knew my dark side as well. Finally, I had the courage to ask God what was my role in Glen's retirement and how should I support him? And God responded by simply saying, "Tell your son's story!"

In Genesis 2:24, God tells us that "a man will leave his father and mother, and shall cleave unto his wife: and they shall be one flesh!"

This verse is so important because many of us leave physically, but we don't leave mentally and spiritually! As parents we have our kids for a season to teach them to serve God. If we keep running to mommy and daddy when a problem occurs, we will never develop the intimate relationship that God wants with Him!

In the Bible, we read about a group of religious leaders known as the Pharisees. The Pharisees knew a lot about God, but they never surrendered their hearts to him!

In this book, Glen and I will show our readers that money does not control us and that we have a relentless pursuit in serving God. We will also show that He truly loves us and is waiting to have an intimate relationship with us! He gave no excuses in relentlessly pursuing us!

Selfishness, pride, and denial devour us daily. Glen gave up millions of dollars to pursue God's love because he respected, feared, and loved God. I'm so grateful that Glen didn't call me and ask for my opinion when he retired from the NFL! I probably would have said, "Can you think about it for about ten years!" LOL. The truth is that I'm not God, and if God talks to your heart, listen to Him. Don't try to get the opinions of the world!

Our hearts are constantly flooded with the influence of the world. Eventually, we have to reckon with everything that we allow into our hearts. The things we pursue will surely catch up with us someday.

This correspondence reflects sharp divergent points of view: some readers admire Glen immensely for his courage and noble decision; others, such as the media and some fans, fulminated that he's a reckless idiot and stupid for not pursuing the fame and millions of dollars.

My convictions will be apparent soon enough, but I'll leave it to the readers to form his or her own opinion of Glenwood Razeem Coffee Jr.

CHAPTER 1

The Birth

My name is Glenwood Coffee Sr. I was born in the small town of New Madrid, Missouri. As I look back at my adolescence, I realize that I had a descent upbringing but somewhat dysfunctional as well. My father passed when I was very young.

A family of the Kingdom that is functionally sound consists of a godly man and woman that are raising godly children. But fear not because our omnipotent God is so loving and merciful. He has left His living word for any of us that lack wisdom and knowledge.

I graduated from Lilbourn High School in 1980. Shortly after graduating high school, I went to Bailey Technical, a technical college in St. Louis, Missouri.

After my second year of college, I realized that I wasn't committed and didn't have the discipline for college.

An Air Force recruiting office was located near my college, and often I would talk to the recruiter there.

Because I wasn't doing so well in school, I decided to take the Air Force enlistment test. And oh, by the way, there was also a girl's college right next to mine, and there was a party every day.

Still today I'm so thankful that the Air Force recruiter encouraged me to take the enlistment test. I grew up and became a godly man in the Air Force.

My first assignment in the Air Force was Torrejon Air Force Base, Spain, and my second assignment was Eglin Air Force Base, Florida. I proudly served eight years in the Air Force. Thank God for Eglin Air Force Base because that's where I got married to Glen's mom and that's where Glen was born as well.

I'll never forget as I witnessed his birth. It was one of the most astonishing blessings that I have ever witnessed. Glen was such a handsome baby boy. He was also a happy baby who never really cried much. I remember how defined and toned his body was when he was around six months old. He looked like a little Hulk baby! Even today he's one of the most conditioned athletes that I know.

I was a typical father, proud and boastful, just beating on my chest, sending a shockwave around the world, chanting, "Look at me and my son!" At the time of Glen's birth, I have to admit that I was basically a fair-weather Christian. I confessed that I was a Christian, but my life didn't reflect the life of a faithful servant.

As I stated earlier in my text, I grew up without a godly male figure in my household. I was supposed to be an extension of my father; and it was his responsibility to teach me how to be a godly man, a father, husband, and potentially a grandfather. Because he passed when I was very young, I grew up with a void and missed out on a whole generation of fatherly guidance.

In reference to marriage, as I look back at my courtship, the process of wooing a potential wife, the hunt was based on my terms instead of God's instructions. In Proverbs 31:10 God tells us men, "Who can find the virtuous woman for her value is more than rubies?" Although our world doesn't acknowledge this fact, God does say that the man should be the head of the household. I do understand that some of us men don't measure up to our part of the bargain. As men, we carry a lot of responsibility on own our shoulders. This is why it's vital that both men and women truly understand their godly role in holy matrimony. People are lost and hurting because they've never had a godly head in their household. How can a man or woman recognize true leadership or true love after never having a godly man or woman shape their life? Money, new houses, and cars can't and never will replace God's love!

This is a plague that infects so many homes!

The seniors that graduate high school, tomorrow's leaders, if they truly had God's message and not the watered-down version embedded in their hearts, can you imagine how our world would be impacted?

When both parties understand their purpose in the relationship, it brings balance and allows them to make needed adjustments, instead of responding from emotions that cripple the relationship.

In the Book of Ephesians, God tells us that marriage should be a symbol of Jesus and the church.

Yes, I got married because I wanted a beautiful woman to give me a handsome son, which God did bless me with Glen! And I'm so, so thankful!

Life should and must be about lessons learned. Please underline and pass this next statement on to your loved ones: marriage is the most important and fulfilling relationship that God has created for men and women! But the first and foremost reason that we should pray for marriage is to find someone to help us serve Jesus! That's it! Nothing more, nothing less!

When we both are on fire for Christ and love Him first. He will show us how to love one another, and everything else will fall into its rightful place! WOW, that's some good word!

Let's take a moment and discuss the term "on fire for Christ!" I'm not necessarily referring to people that go to church every Sunday or people that wear the best suits, or even people that drive the newest cars. Attending church is very important, but some people go to church for all the wrong reasons!

People that are on fire for Christ aren't perfect; but they believe, fear, trust, and love Him with all their mind, body, and soul!

A part of me trembles as I look back because I realize that I wasn't prepared as much as I should have been to bring a child into this world. As a parent, even if you do all the right things in raising your children, which I did not, you just don't know how your children will turn out.

Children are so precious and a gift from God. They're not pets. You can't give them back if you don't want to feed them or care for them.

In Proverbs 22:6 God tells us "to train a child in the way he should go: and when he is old he will not depart from it."

When Glen was around four years old, we moved to New Orleans, Louisiana, because I separated from the Air Force and took a job with the New Orleans International Airport.

Glen really liked New Orleans. Because his mom and I both worked, he would go to a day-care facility. Glen liked his day care because he had plenty of new friends to play with all day long. And, of course one of Glen's favorite times of the day was his lunch period where he was served peanut butter and jelly sandwiches every day. And to this day, we still laugh and joke about the (PBJ) sandwiches.

CHAPTER 2

Growing Up in Saudi Arabia

Glen was around four years old when we moved to Saudi Arabia with my wife at the time, Doris, and his younger brother Matt.

Due to my technical college and military training, I qualified for an engineering position with Boeing Aerospace. Saudi would be our home for six years, and it was new and exciting. I think Glen and his brother liked Saudi more than I did.

It's so amazing how our bodies adapt to different environments. I remember when I first arrived in Saudi Arabia. The plane landed, and as I walked down the stairs of the plane, it was so hot I could barely breath! My first assumption was that the unbearable heat was from the engine exhaust. I would soon realize that it was just a typical 120-degree day in Saudi!

I was in the country six months prior to Doris and the boys coming over, and I was so excited to reunite with them and show them their new world.

The flight time from New York to Saudi is around thirteen hours (nonstop), so you can imagine how exhausted they were when they arrived.

So Saudi Arabia would be the home for the Coffee family. I didn't really realize it, but there were so many blessings waiting for us on that journey.

If you think about it, Saudi Arabia is not on the top ten vacation list. When we took our yearly thirty-day paid vacation back to America, we'd get some weird looks from our friends and family when we told them that we lived in Saudi Arabia.

There is so much biblical history in the Middle East. The crossing of the Red Sea is part of the biblical narrative of the escape of the Israelites, led by Moses, from the pursuing Egyptians in the book of Exodus13:17–14:29.

The Red Sea is the boundary and separates Africa from Saudi Arabia. I remember watching the Discovery Channel where a zebra walked right in front of a lion in the heat of the day and the lion just sat in the shade relaxing like the zebra wasn't even there! Due to the unbearable heat during the day, the lions would hunt in the cool of the night.

I'm not going to deny that life in Saudi is vastly different from our life in America. All things considered, I would like to let the rest of the world know that, with an open mind and sense of adventure, life in Saudi Arabia can be pretty awesome!

Most Western expats come to Saudi Arabia for one reason: money!

Being a former Air Force boxer and current fitness trainer, I was so grateful to discover that softball, soccer, Little League Baseball, and racquetball were very popular in our new home.

Landing a position in Saudi as an experienced and educated professional typically came with perks that jobs back home didn't offer. Generous tax-free salaries, free luxurious housing, paid education for your children, free tickets back home, and don't mention the minimum standard of thirty-day paid vacation are all benefits offered to Western expats!

The rent-free villa that we lived in had eight bathrooms and the carpet was three-inches thick. We lived the life of the royal family. Because we lived in that region of the world, our vacations consisted of Amsterdam, Thailand, Bahrain, United Emirates, etc., which truly opened our eyes to the real world, not propaganda.

I'm compelled to comment on the concept of breaking bread. Bread is still cooked the same way when Jesus walked the earth in Saudi Arabia—in stone ovens.

There are dozens of verses in the Bible in relation to breaking bread. Prior to living in Saudi, I never envisioned bread being the main ingredient of a meal. Me, being a witness, I totally understand how the bread in Saudi truly has a biblical purpose. It's so fulfilling. I have eaten at several Saudi diners where bread is the main source of food, and it is so good.

I'm so thankful that God created and allowed us to play sports. Sports unite our segregated worlds! Sports truly helped me forge even a greater relationship with my boys!

I had the pleasure of coaching Glen in soccer and baseball in Saudi! As a parent, I feel that we should try to expose our children to as many activities as possible and evaluate how they respond.

Of course, soccer is the most popular sport in Saudi Arabia. Glen showed tremendous interest in soccer and quickly became very crafty playing it. He would kick a pass to himself by dribbling the ball with the crowd, then he would kick the ball toward the goalie and explode from the rest of the players and position himself to where it would be only him and the goalie. At this point he would deliver a monstrous kick to where one would think the soccer ball was going to penetrate the net!

After playing several games, Glen's competitive reputation spread very quickly and some goalies would just move away to avoid the impact of Glen's ball.

Coaching baseball was slightly challenging but tons of fun as well. One of my biggest challenges was trying to keep the kids focused. Anytime that the players were in line or in the dugout, they would talk, talk, talk or hit each other. You know, the things kids do at that age. To build discipline, I would tell the players, "If I see anyone talking and not paying attention, you're going to run the bases!"

One day I designed a plan of attack to combat the talking and the not-paying-attention issue. I pulled Glen to the side and said, "Son, I need your help. We've got a good team, and you're one of the leaders!"

He replied, "Okay, Dad. What do you want me to do?"

So, I said, "I want you guys to listen and pay attention. You guys don't like to lose games, right? If you listen more, we'll win more, okay? So in order to get everyone's attention, while you all are talking, I'm going to call you out with a loud voice. 'Glen, are you talking?' Then I'll say, 'Get out there and run those bases!'"

So, Glen said, "Okay, Dad, I understand. Let's do it!"

So, we resumed practice and executed our plan. Glen went to the dugout, and of course, everyone was talking and playing around. I suddenly yelled out with a deep voice that sent a shockwave around the field, "Glen, are you guys talking? What did I just say?" Before he could answer, I yelled, "RUN THOSE BASES!"

Glen played his role really well. He had an expression on his face as if he was really in trouble, and he ran hard, touching every base!

So when Glen came back to the dugout, I said, "Now that's how you run the bases!"

We did capture the team's attention for about a whole five minutes, then they continued talking and playing again!

Amazingly, our games were very exciting and packed with fun.

One bad habit that we tried to combat and prevent the kids from doing was watching where the ball would land after they hit it. We coached them to run regardless, not stand and watch it.

One game Glen was at bat, and it was the end of the ninth inning. There were two outs, and we had a runner on first, the score was 4–3. The other team was up. Glen was the best athlete and hitter on the team, I asked him, "Okay, son, are you ready?" He responded, "Yeah, Dad!" So he wound up, and the pitcher pitched the ball. Glen swung the bat like he was in one of the World Series baseball games! I knew he hit the ball very well! The ball went so high in the air to the point that we could barely see it! And, of course, we were all yelling, "Run, run, and run, run." And, of course, Glen was planted there at home plate just gazing up in the sky, trying to locate his ball. Our runner on first was planted, gazing as well!

It seemed like the ball was in the air for an eternity! Finally, the ball came tumbling down and landed behind second base. Then Glen decided to explode to first base, and our runner on first headed to second. But it was too late. Our runner on first was easily tagged out! As adults we have to love the effort that the players are giving, and the excitement that the game brings.

As coaches our main goal was to build character in our players and teach them the value of respect, responsibility, caring, honesty, and faith. At some point in a child's life, the pressure of winning or losing should not be the main topic! Having fun is what's going to keep that child wanting to come back.

Of course, when they get older, the coaching scheme will change and their objective will change. That's why it's so important for a child to have a chance to simply enjoy the game and be a kid!

Although Glen mastered soccer and baseball in Saudi Arabia, American football was always his passion. Unfortunately, there was no organized American football played in Saudi Arabia. So Glen and his friends would play pick-up football in the streets, on the concrete, every day! Our community was safe and clean, and all of the kids that lived there played street football. It was definitely a symbol of an American passion!

CHAPTER 3

Coming to America

We had lived in Saudi Arabia for six years, and Saudi had been very good to our family. Our compound was an international community. We had friends from all over the world living there. Glen and his friends were very close, and it was extremely hard saying good-bye to them. So we said our good-byes, and the moving company came and packed our belongings and prepared them for shipment.

I was responsible for gathering and maintaining everyone's passport, so after accounting for tickets and all other traveling documents, we made our way to the Dhahran International Airport!

The airport really gives you a snapshot of the diversity in the Middle East. We were in the mist of so many different cultures. Just looking around in the airport I could see the Egyptians, Indians, Ethiopians, Pakistani, Filipinos, Turkish, Nepalese, Koreans, Lebanese, and the list goes on and on.

We are privileged today to live in a world of many cultures. The Bible verses on culture diversity lets us know that it's really something we notice more than God.

Can you imagine how boring this world would be if we all looked the same, smell the same, and taste the same? LOL.

A diverse functional world is one that values inclusion and differences in people. It is one that recognizes that people with different backgrounds bring different gifts, skills, attitudes, experiences, and fresh ideas. Studies show that lack of cohesion between races, sexes, and cultures is due to mistrust, stereotyping, segregation, abuse, and racism!

Some ethnic groups even feel they are superior over others for whatever reason. For example, in the Webster dictionary, you will find the worldly definition of racism. It states, "prejudice, discrimination or antagonism directed against someone of a different race on the belief that one's race is superior."

This definition is misleading and keeps the human race at bay!

The godly definition for racism is simply the absence of God in one's life! The true reality of life is Jesus or Satan, and we will serve one or the other!

This is what God says about our cultural differences in Mark 12:31: "You shall love your neighbor as yourself." There is no other commandment greater than this!

I was so proud of my family. We had moved to a foreign land; and we adapted, lived, and flourished. I remember prior to coming to Saudi how some family and friends tried to convince me not to pursue the tremendous opportunity! I realize that their motives were based from fear and ignorance! We miss out on so many opportunities because of fear. And opportunity doesn't go away; it simply goes to someone else!

Fear is not part of our character. It's a tool used by the adversary to keep us in bondage!

In Genesis 3:9–10 God shows us the origin of fear and how we respond to it: "And the Lord God called unto Adam, and said unto him, 'Where art thou?' And he said, 'I heard thy voice in the garden and I was afraid because I was naked; and I hid myself!'"

Not only does fear threaten our emotions, it also causes changes in our metabolic and organ functions, which ultimately changes our behavior.

So we finally arrived back in America after a long tasking trip. Our itinerary was Dhahran, Saudi Arabia, to New York (JFK) to Atlanta (ATL) to Fort Walton Beach, Florida (VPS). We were all so happy to return home!

We had rented our home and made plans for it to be vacant upon our return.

Thank God our house was in pretty good shape. We had only minor repairs. After getting settled in our home, the next biggest task was enrolling the boys in school.

We were so excited about being back in America, our home, the greatest country in the world! There are so many beautiful attractions raging from the Statue of Liberty in New York to the Grand Canyon in Arizona or the Golden Gate Bridge in San Francisco.

We finally enrolled Glen into school, but one of our concerns was that he often talked about bullying and peer pressure that occurred at his school.

Glen was ten years old and in the fourth grade. I realized Glen always had friends because he was very active and he was so competitive in sports. Kids are always looking for ways to be compatible and fit in with their peers.

In Saudi the topic of peer pressure never really surfaced. I knew we were a smaller community and the fact that we were Americans living in a foreign land maybe encouraged us to be more family oriented.

I sat down and talked to Glen about bullying, how it affected him and how he felt about it. He said that he had several classmates who were very good friends that interacted well in sports and other activities. However, the kids who were shy or timid were constantly being attacked physically, verbally, or by being excluded socially.

I told Glen that he should care for and respect everyone and not participate or support anyone with aggressive behavior.

Unfortunately, all young people are in danger of being bullied at some point during their adolescence.

There are many factors that may influence offensive and aggressive behavior in youth. I feel the most important one is family situations.

In the Bible God shows us the importance of spiritual disciplines. He tells us that discipline is not part of the sin nature but is a natural part of the Christian life. Spiritual discipline can be described as those behaviors that augment our spiritual growth and enable us to grow to spiritual maturity.

God tells us that selfish pride is excessive confidence or glorification in one's self. Also along with pride itself, words such as *arrogance*, *haughtiness*, and *conceit* are all opposite of godly humility.

This is what the apostle Paul says about our true nature and how we should conduct ourselves: Love is a consequence of faith in God. When we have sufficient faith and trust in God, the Holy Spirit gives us the gift of love as a sign of what's to come in the Kingdom of God. Love is thus not a product of human thought or emotions; it's not possible for mere humans to experience genuine love. Love is a divine gift that occurs only when we allow Christ to live within us.

Thus, do some Christians insist that nonbelievers don't really know what love is?

CHAPTER 4

City League Football and Bruner

City League Football is a rich tradition growing up in the state of Florida. First, I'd like to say that City League Football still falls into the category of youth sports! What defines youth sports? Well, youth sports should be a place where kids can learn, grow, develop, and have fun.

The sad fact is that too often parents are yelling at the officials, and bad sportsmanship is being allowed on the field. Instead of this being a healthy and educational environment, sometimes it becomes a toxic one!

Thank God for coaches who really want to give back to the community without hidden agendas.

Coaching is sometimes a thankless, frustrating kind of job. It's an occupation that is often done in the light of public view where you're constantly being exposed and evaluated.

When it comes to judging your performance, everyone seems to be an expert and have the qualifications to criticize you.

Most of your coaching ability is measured by winning or losing, and it's totally unfair when you're coaching nine-, ten-, and eleven-year-old kids!

Mr. Brian was Glen's coach, and winning was not his main objective! His number one goal was to get the players to believe in themselves by building them up rather than knocking them down.

In the City League environment, in relation to recruiting players, a coach really doesn't have any control over the talent level as he builds his roster.

You would think that most coaches would want parity across the league and not let their egos and self-worth get tied up in the outcome of the game.

Well, finally Coach Brian had his parent-coaches meeting, and he assured us that his priority was to build character first!

He continued by saying that not only will he teach fundamentals, but also look for opportunities where important life lessons can be taught, such as mastering hardship and handling and rebounding from failures and setbacks and also trusting your teammates, emotionally dealing with winning and losing, good sportsmanship, respect, responsibility, etc.

As a parent I was relieved to hear his coaching scheme and even more impressed to see that he led by example!

Yes, we know that the players are a reflection of their parents and also the parents are a reflection of the coach. Coach Brian was very humble and appreciative. Both parents and players got along well.

Glen's practices went very well. After evaluating his players, coach Brian begin to assign roles based on performances and natural ability.

Coach Brian needed someone to fill the running back position. The traits that make a quality power running back is the ability to run with a low center of gravity, which is an advantage when engaging the opposition, also being a balanced ball carrier, mental toughness, and strength to run with power to penetrate the defensive line.

Due to his relentless pursuit and hard work on the field, Glen was awarded the running back position. The name of Glen's team was the Florida Gators. After playing pick-up and tackle football for all those years in Saudi Arabia, Glen finally had his debut to play organized football!

Glen's first game was very impressive and entertaining. He ran with great confidence and authority, finishing with eighty yards and two touchdowns. After each game Coach Brian would rally the troops. They would take a knee, and he would pray and thank God for a fun, safe game.

An innocent, blameless, moral, decent prayer with values more than gold. Fellowship comes from the Greek word *KOINONIA*, which means "to share in common." Christian fellowship is more than attending church; it is assimilating into the body of believers, becoming one in worshipping, loving, caring, and sharing.

Keep in mind, salvation is based on faith, not earned by performing works such as attending church (Eph. 2:8–9). But fellowship with Christ's body, the church, is critical in helping sustain your faith by providing ministry, encouragement, and an atmosphere of spiritual cleaning and growth.

Going to church, praying, fellowshipping, and reading the Bible are all part of the relationship with Christ. For some of the players on Glen's team, that prayer was their church because they didn't go to church and there wasn't a godly influence in their home.

I know those prayers helped me. Because of work, often I wouldn't attend church. That's why God is so AWESOME. He always provides multiple outlets where we can plug in to receive his mighty word!

I'm very proud of Glen. He adapted very well in the City League environment. He was on every coach's radar as being one of the top players in the league. We didn't realize it at that moment, but the Gators would deliver an undefeated, dominant performance under Coach Brian for two seasons.

Glen was an awesome role model for his younger brother Matt. While Glen was on the field performing, Matt developed a love for the game and became a gifted football player as well.

Matt went on to earn a scholarship to the University of South Carolina and played for legendary coach Steve Spurrier.

Glen was twelve years old, and it was time for him to head to middle school and play middle school football. Bruner Middle School was in our school district, and Glen would attend his sixth, seventh, and eighth grades there. Being part of the City League Football family helped Glen's transition to Bruner because he had played with or against so many of the new students.

Of the 974 middle schools in the state of Florida, Max Bruner is ranked number 310, which is pretty good. Max Bruner Middle School, Land of the Spartans, are very competitive academically and had the most successful football program in Okaloosa County.

Since Glen's former City League coach had delivered two championship seasons, I was eager to meet Glen's coaching staff at Bruner. His new coaches were Coach Vincent and Coach Bowman. I finally got a chance to meet them after their first practice, and wow, they gave me an earful of the expectations of the players and parents.

I have to admit that I was very impressed with their strategy. They both were dynamic and passionate, and their coaching record spoke for itself. Their conversations were so engaging and addictive that you could easily talk the night away.

At this point anticipations and expectations were at their highest, a complete veteran team with two of the best coaches in the football arena.

As I look back, I realize now that this is when I got caught up in the hype of Glen's stardom. Meaning, I was becoming too much of a fan than a prudent father.

Coaches teach their players to challenge themselves and overcome adversity. If you fall, figure out why, get up, and try it again. Persistence translates to results.

The players are physically prepared in the weight room; mentally prepared by studying film, play books, and coaching schemes; and spiritually prepared by staying on their knees praying to God before and after games.

These same principles are very appropriate and should be applied in the classroom, when applying for a job, while studying God's word, and in everyday life. If the human race would even remotely apply these principles of fundamental football, it would increase everyone's success rate!

Ephesians 1:3–5 tells us, "All praises to God, the father of our Lord Jesus Christ, who has blessed us with every blessing in the heavenly realm because we are united with Christ!" As Christians we should expect our children to be very successful. It's great for our children to have goals and dream big. As parents we need to be visionaries and have even a bigger vision to show our children all their potential.

The more Glen played, the more compliments I got. And I started becoming his fan. When I would talk to him about his grades in school, the touchdowns would trump the Bs and Cs. Glen was extremely smart. He would make As on test with virtually no preparation, but he would fail to turn in homework and would have to settle for Bs and Cs instead.

At the City League and middle school level, I don't think the audience really understands the importance of a stout defensive scheme.

Although touchdowns wins game, a defensive-minded coach win championships. If your defense is constant and you can count on shutting your opponent down in key situations, you will win a lot of games even if your offense isn't as talented.

Coach Vincent was a defensive specialist that mastered the ability to get his defensive players fired up! In some ways defensive players have to be better athletes in order to pressure the quarterback to stop the deep ball or stop the running back in the backfield for a loss.

A successful football program translates to a successful strength and conditioning program for both offense and defense.

The Spartans would take the field and deliver a beautiful array of strength, speed, agility, endurance, and explosiveness, a direct reflection of their dedication in the weight room.

I remember the first Spartan game, after a big defensive hit, Coach Vincent would shout, "Look at the hit. He just put a 'hat' on that dude," referring to the big hit! Then he would start jumping up and down so fast causing the whole sideline to erupt. Even I wanted to suit up and beg him to put me in the game!

Having a military background, I took an oath to serve this country with my life, no exceptions! Seeing the Spartans operate on the field was a true reflection of a military unit, each dedicated to their role, understanding that if anyone misses an assignment that it would jeopardize the whole play!

The Spartans main offense was the *I* formation, aligned with the quarter, fullback, and running back. Glen's fullback was a big stout football player named Ralph Ousley, and they were virtually unstoppable!

In a typical offensive play, the quarterback would snap the ball, hand it to Glen, and he would follow his fullback or plow through the right guard and right tackle!

The time with Coach Vincent was another very successful experience for Glen. He broke several records at Bruner, some still current even today.

I was on the Air Force boxing team in Madrid, Spain, for several years; so I would train with Glen and Matt quiet often. I knew he was a herald athlete, but I had no idea that he was freakishly blessed with a set of fast twitch muscles that would help him land a state weight meet title his senior year.

So many blessings came out of the Spartan era. Years later Bruner Middle School retired Glen's jersey, and I proudly accepted it on his behalf.

When you walk into the Spartan's weight room, number 24 is proudly displayed. Glen has truly left a positive legacy for his fellow Spartans.

Glen played three years at Bruner Middle School with an undefeated record of 24–0! I will always cherish the days of the Spartans because Coach Vincent was a praying coach. He loved and believed in all his players. As parents we conformed to his world!

CHAPTER 5

The Vikings

Wow, Glen is a freshman at Fort Walton Beach High School. The dynamics of high school are much different than elementary or middle school. Glen really had to learn the importance of time management. He quickly needed to learn how to prioritize his time in and outside of the classroom.

College may seem far off at this point, but college scouts look at all four years of a potential candidate that would possibly earn a scholarship at their university.

At this point in Glen's life he conducted an assessment of his football career. He told himself that "I'm bigger, faster, and stronger than most of the athletes my age. And I know I can make it to the NFL." So Glen vowed from that day on that his number one purpose in life was to make it to the NFL.

With elementary and middle school behind him now, Glen had played five consecutive years without losing a football game. Now he was a freshman on the Fort Walton Beach junior varsity football team and would soon suffer the agony of defeat!

When losses start occurring, self-doubt is sure to follow, but Glen was a self-motivator and worked very hard on the football field.

He instinctively knew that he had to continue to hustle, be enthusiastic, and bring energy to the practice field to motivate his teammates.

When you as a parent sit down and talk to your child about losing, most of the time their response is a reflection of your value system. Frustration, anger, disappointment, and embarrassment are all feelings that stir up when losing is the topic.

It's not easy to accept defeat, nor to endure the embarrassment and shame that comes along with it. Everyone hates to see their team or child lose.

There is a degree of loyalty to which some fans go that is far beyond any right enjoyment in sports and any right delight in their teams. Getting frustrated over a loss is understandable. Reacting with bitterness, hurt, and rage over that loss, however, is idolatry.

In Paul's second letter to the Corinthians, he spoke about how acknowledging our weakness makes room for Christ's power. "I will boast all the more gladly about my weakness, so that Christ's power may rest on me. That is why, for Christ sake, I delight in weakness… for when I am weak, and then I am strong (2 Cor. 12:9–10).

In today's world our walk with Christ is totally opposite compared to Paul's faith. We hind behind our titles, giving a false impression that we don't have any weakness and that our world is perfect, yet Paul openly shares his weakness!

I missed most of Glen's junior varsity games because my job took me back to Saudi Arabia on a solo tour for a year or so! When I'd talk to Glen about school and simply to check on things, our conversation would either begin with football or end with football. He told me that he wanted to be bigger and stronger. I knew he was very dedicated in the weight room, so I asked him about his eating habits to make sure that he was getting proper nutrition!

I told Glen and Matt that they both should be eating whole foods that is close to its natural form and minimize the consumption of chemically processed foods. Chemically processed foods are usually loaded with sugar or its evil twin, high-fructose corn syrup. Sugar has no essential nutrients. It's an empty calorie.

Many studies show that sugar can have devastating effects on metabolism. High sugar consumption is strongly paired with some of the world's leading killers, including heart disease, diabetes, obesity, and cancer.

I really wanted to infuse this topic and paint a picture about the importance of our bodies getting proper nutrition.

I completed my second tour in Saudi Arabia with Boeing Aerospace, and it was time to head home. I was really excited to see everyone. Glen and Matt looked really well. Their mom did a great job with them.

Glen was a junior in high school when I arrived back home, and it was football season. I have to admit that he had a very good growth spurt going on. He was around six feet and weighed around 190 pounds. Even his voice had a deeper tone. Last but not least, he was packing some serious muscle tone. I almost felt the need to ask him if I could have my house back. I did tell him that he was the man of the house while I was gone.

During your teen years, you're in a phase of your life when your body wants to grow. You're churning out hormones that are specially designed to help you get bigger.

To stay focused on the task at hand, we immediately implemented Glen's nutrition plan. Lack of proper nutrition is a plague that hunts so many children in America. Eighty percent of what determines an athlete's performance is the quality of their nutrition.

Once again, no sodas or fast foods! First, a good breakfast is a vital meal that sets your energy and metabolism for the rest of the day. If you're an athlete seven day of the week, you eat like an athlete seven day of the week.

Football is a stop-and-go sport with short bursts of intense effort, followed by rest. Therefore, the primary fuel for football is carbohydrates!

An ideal diet for football players requires 55 to 60 percent of their daily caloric intake to come from carbohydrates, 15 percent from protein, and 30 percent from fat.

Carbohydrates-containing foods with lower fat should be emphasized. For example, bagels over doughnuts, mashed potatoes over fries, grilled chicken over fried, frozen yogurt over ice cream.

Upping the amount of carbohydrates in your diet will provide you with more available energy during practice and games. During dinnertime I would cook healthy dinners for Glen, consisting of baked, boiled, or grilled foods.

Knowing boxers are some of the most conditions athletes on the planet, Glen would often ask me about my experience when I fought for the Air Force. I wanted Glen to understand that boxing and I were one flesh, as in a marriage. I was totally committed. I went to bed boxing, dreamed boxing, and got up boxing! A typical day for me consisted of getting up at 5:00 a.m., run six miles, shower, eat breakfast, then go back to sleep, get up at noon, eat lunch, then train from 2:00 p.m. to 6:00 p.m., shower, then eat dinner and go to bed. The next day we'd get up and do it all over again!

Most importantly I wanted Glen to understand that maintaining optimal zest of life should be for a lifetime. Unfortunately, I've watched friends and family members struggle due to lack of proper nutrition and a sedentary lifestyle!

This is what God says about our bodies in 1 Corinthians 6:19–20, "What know ye not that your body is the temple of the Holy Ghost which is in you, which ye have of God, and ye are not your own? For ye are bought with a price: therefore glorify God in your body, and in your spirit which are Gods!" WOW. In these verses, the apostle Paul is telling us that our bodies don't even belong to us, it's a gift from God. Therefore honoring our bodies as sacred temples certainly includes eating healthy foods that keep them functioning well.

Glen had a good junior year playing football for the Fort Walton Beach Vikings. He was the second string running back and shared carries with the starting senior back. He finished his junior year with 825 rushing and 275 receiving yards and 10 touchdowns. Yes, Glen's stats were good, but we knew they weren't good enough to have college scouts knocking at our door.

It was hard to imagine, but Glen was headed into his last year of high school, his last homecoming, last prom, and, eventually, his last football game!

To stay on target Glen identified three areas of focus that would give him the breakthrough season his last year of high school football.

First, he knew that he needed to work harder academically and bring his GPA up and also to continue to work hard in the weight room and get proper nutrition. Last was to participate in as many football camps as possible!

Thank God Glen's stats were good enough to get him invites to a Nike Camp with the LSU Tigers and another camp in the swamp with the Florida Gators!

The Nike Football Training Camps are designed to help elite high school football players with college potential advance their football and training knowledge in order to maximize their ability. The players will have an opportunity to work with SPARQ trainers that have molded stars such as Deion Sanders, Walter Jones, Calvin Johnson, Derrick Brooks, and many more.

Athletes who come to the Nike Football Training Camp will register, where they will pick up their free Nike Pro workout shirt and get their photo taken.

After a proper, supervised dynamic warm-up, trainers work participants through specific drills designed to improve athletic ability, speed, and explosiveness.

Position-specific drills separate the participants into position groups (QBs, RBs, WR/TEs, OLS and DBs) to work individually on football skills and techniques with top-notch position coaches with college and NFL experience.

One-on-ones conclude with one-on-one passing and noncontact line drills, which many say are the highlight of the camp.

Video and action photos for ESPN and other national media will be taken. Participants will also be part of the in-depth coverage on ESPN.com, ESPNRISE.com, and ESPNU. Glen was competing against 250 prospects! I knew Glen was 100 percent healthy.

The perseverance, self-denial, hard work, and sacrifice would allow Glen to unleash an epic performance! Glen's amazing frame, great footwork, and soft hands out of the back field would give him MVP honors! Glen earned two MVP honors. He had the highest spark rating in the workout drills and earned MVP in the 7-on-7 drills as well, which gave him an overall high rating and set his stock plunging through the roof!

Glen bench pressed 185 pounds 22 times, ran a 4.44 forty, and had a vertical leap of 36 inches!

He had received some scholarship offers to play college football from his junior year. Immediately after the Nike Camp, the offer letters stared piling up because they were coming in so fast!

Coach Nick Saban was the head football coach for the LSU Tigers at the time of Glen's Nike Camp experience. Shortly after the camp, Coach Saban invited the top twenty-five prospects back to LSU along with their parents. Former LSU coach Will Muschanp was our representative upon arrival. He assisted us with any questions and gave us a tour of Tiger Stadium! And, of course, we were very excited for Glen and his potential opportunity to play for LSU! We were also very excited to meet legendary coach Saban!

Prior to our interview with Coach Saban, we had the opportunity to mingle and meet some of the prospects.

For me, it was a bittersweet moment. I was excited for all the invites, and I was in the midst of some of the most gifted, talented athletes in the nation. The sad part for me was that these were young men and some of them were borderline disrespectful. Their pants were hanging down to the ground, chains hung to their waste, no eye contact. Some didn't even want to shake my hand, giving me a cold impression that in their eyes they were already famous!

I totally supported Coach Saban's approach and his interviewing process with the prospects and their parents. Great coaches not only prepare their players to win championships, they also prepare their players to be winners in life!

In our interview with Coach Saban, I felt that he was a very genuine coach without hidden agendas. He elaborated on a very competitive academic program at LSU, state-of-the-art training facility for the players, and a very impressive winning tradition for the LSU Tigers!

I was totally sold on Coach Saban's proposal, but it would be Glen's decision on what school he would attend. Coach Saban provided so much information, it was a lot to process, and the thoughts in my mind were racing 100 miles per hour! There was one question that I wanted to ask him, but there was never a pause in his briefing. There was a rumor floating around that he may elect to coach for the Miami Dolphins, so I kind of interrupted him and asked him if he was considering leaving college and coach in the NFL.

So he paused and gave me the look! I've seen him go ballistic and chew out his on coaching staff during the game! My focus was Glen. I really liked Coach Saban and hoped that it was just a rumor about him possibly leaving LSU.

Thankfully, Coach Saban answered very respectfully and said he had no intentions of pursuing the NFL! I assume Coach Saban got an offer that he couldn't refuse because he did go coach for the

Miami Dolphins. It worked out well for us anyway because LSU wanted Glen to play strong safety and Glen was a running back!

We didn't know it at the time, but fate would bring Coach Saban back into Glen's football life in a big way!

So now the camp is over, and it was time for Glen to get back to Fort Walton Beach to hit the practice field.

Glen had offers from Maryland, Louisville, UCF, Southern Miss, Middle Tennessee, West Virginia, etc. These were all blessings, but Glen was a Florida native and his dreams were to play with Miami, Florida State, or the Florida Gators. I told him to stay prayed up as he still had his senior year of football left.

Glen's high school football coach was Mike Owens. Because I was the associate branch director for the Emerald Coast YMCA, I would collaborate with all coaches in my county to help with my youth sports programs.

I remember watching Glen practice in the steamy August conditions. It was a grind, but they all enjoyed getting out there competing.

Anytime I would come watch Glen practice, Coach Owens would purposely run plays designed for him so I could evaluate his production. If Glen came out of the backfield with the ball or received a pass, he would literally transform into a beast-like figure and explode down the field just hoping someone would try to tackle him! Glen's motto was "I'd rather run through you than waste time running around you!"

The Vikings had a very successful practice season with minimal injuries. Now it was time for their first game, which was a kickoff classic in Navarre, Florida, a neighboring town.

At that time Rivals.com had Glen ranked number 3 in the state of Florida.

Knowing that he was coaching one of the most decorated backs in the country, Coach Owens and his staff designed a secret plan of attack to only play Glen if they needed him for the kickoff classic!

It was the first football game of Glen's senior year. The pep rallies, marching bands, and mascots are at full bloom; and he was not even on the field!

It was a clever coaching scheme on Coach Owens part to rest Glen, but Glen wasn't aware of it. I was near the sideline and kind of gestured at Glen, like "What's going on?" He gestured back, "I don't have a clue?"

Navarre won the coin toss and elected to receive the ball to start the game. They handed the ball off and marched down the field and scored. The Vikings started out with a pass and the receiver gained around fifty yards. The next play was a running play and the backup running back took the ball into the end zone for a touchdown.

The second quarter is a defensive battle. No team scored, and we closed the first half with a tied score of 7–7! At this point I was thinking Glen may not play in the opening game.

So the third quarter started, and surprisingly number 8 Glen Coffee was in the end zone waiting to receive the kickoff!

Glen received the ball on the ten-yard line, patiently followed his blocks, broke a tackle at the thirty-yard line, broke another tackle at the fifty-yard line, then he just relied on his open-field running ability; and within a blink of the eye, he was in the end zone! WOW, a ninety-yard return! It happened so fast! It seemed like a delayed reaction. After the Viking fans realized Glen had scored, the whole stadium erupted in an outbreak of pandemonium!

After Glen's ninety-yard return, Coach Owens took him out and he didn't play the remainder of the game. Glen's elegant display of talent was history in the making and that would be his trademark throughout his whole senior year with the Vikings!

The Vikings won their kickoff classic 24–7! Glen would lead the Vikings to the third round of the playoffs that season, lacking only one game that would have taken them to the state finals!

Glen definitely accomplished the breakthrough season he had envisioned. He finished his senior season with dominating stats, which consisted of 2,244 total yards and 30 touchdowns! To sugar coat his resume, Glen also captured the state weight meet title by bench pressing 390 pounds, clean and jerked 305 pounds in the 199-weight division!

During the football season, I would talk to Glen and Coach Owens about his grades in school. Unfortunately, his grades had gotten worse! Glen's GPA had gone from a 2.8 to a 2.0, and it was all based on a lack of effort on Glen's part! Glen scored a 24 on his SAT, which is decent, but some colleges are not going to offer a scholarship to someone with a 2.0 GPA because they just don't know if they're going to graduate.

As a father to son relationship, Glen was a blessing to me. He was very respectable, never in any trouble. He didn't even date until the later part of his junior year. The problem was that my efforts were ineffective in encouraging Glen to transfer his competitive edge from the football field to the classroom!

At this point I felt lost in my own home and walked with guilt for some time!

This was a perfect time for me to minister to Glen and say, "Son, Jesus pursuit for us was never subpar. Jesus gave an all-star performance in everything that he did, and he loved us so much that he died for us!"

The boys and I would have family Bible study, and we would go to church sometimes, but that intimate, unconditional relationship with Christ wasn't where it needed to be for me. At that point in my life I had started to substitute creations for the Creator, not giving God all the glory that he deserved!

February is signing month for all potential signees that will get scholarships, and signing day is approaching fast but still no offers from the Florida Gators, Florida State, or Miami!

Finally, Mickey Andrews from Florida State came to Fort Walton and met with Glen. The meeting was a great confidence builder, but still no confirmed offer.

So one day the mail comes in, and we notice an offer letter from the University of Alabama! Glen's mom jumps with joy and screams, "Glen, you got a letter from Alabama!" We noticed that Glen's response was delayed, and he had a disappointed look on his face because he felt he had earned the right to play for a Florida team! West Virginia had offered Glen, and he was considering playing for them.

After praying and meditating on the possibility of playing for Alabama, Glen told himself that Alabama is in the Southeastern Conference, which is the best conference in college football. So Glen gave Alabama a verbal and inevitably signed with Bama!

Glen's dominating performance on the football field had made him a hometown hero, so when he signed with Alabama, our hometown paper, *The Dailey News*, printed a very nice article in the newspaper and the whole community applauded and embraced him.

Mike Shula was the head coach when Glen initially signed with Alabama, and our friends would joke and asked me if I was going to make Coach Shula wash the dishes or vacuum the floor!

Coach Shula came by our home and provided tons of information about Alabama's football program and assured us that Glen was in good hands. One thing that stood out was that the recruiting cycle is never-ending and it's serious business. Coach Shula informed us that signees commit and de-commit all the time and wanted to make sure the Coffee family was on board.

And, no, I didn't make Coach Shula wash the dishes!

Glen was the first of four running backs to commit to Alabama and assured everyone that he was coming to compete for the starting position!

CHAPTER 6

Freshman at the University of Alabama

We were so grateful to watch Glen walk across the stage to receive his high school diploma! We bought him a very nice car for his graduation present. After all the hard work, Glen had been rewarded by earning a student-athlete scholarship to one of the most prestigious colleges in the nation.

A student-athlete scholarship is the most beneficial, accommodating scholarship that exist, not only is your tuition paid in full, the athletes also get an allowance.

Of course, we would miss Glen and part of me didn't want him to leave for college, but through God's admonishment, I totally understood his destiny. Some households are in turmoil when kids leave for college. Some parents are very possessive and persuade their kids to stay home. Mature parents understand that they only have their children for a season. When that season is over, we must encourage our adult children to really pursue God first in all chooses.

The greatest role model that exist is Jesus Christ. As parents, we're afraid to remind our children that we have issues as well and sometimes we make mistakes also. Jesus became flesh and lived among us sin free!

The world needs true leaders. Holding on to your adult children and keeping them home physically or mentally will cripple them. One report claimed that 89 percent of adult children claim they suffer from long-term relationships with their parents.

We gave Glen our blessings and sent him on his way to Tuscaloosa, Alabama!

By enrolling at Alabama, Glen would be following the footsteps of some of the most influential leaders of our country.

Bear Bryant, Dabo Swinney, Ozzie Newsome, Jim Nabors, Joe Namath, Julio Jones, Mark Ingram, Mike Shula, Shaun Alexander are all alumni of the University of Alabama.

The University of Alabama is a major, comprehensive, student-centered research university found in 1831 as Alabama's first public college.

The university is ranked no. 103 in national universities. The Alabama Crimson Tide Football program represents the University of Alabama in the sport of American football!

I spent most of my adolescent years growing up in Missouri, so I really didn't understand the rich football dynasty of the Southeastern Conference. Glen was getting ready to inherit the most storied and decorated football programs in NCAA history!

Hall of Fame Coach Paul "Bear" Bryant won six National Championships and thirteen Conference Championships for the Crimson Tide. The Paul W. Bryant Museum, Paul W. Bryant Hall, Paul W. Bryant Drive, and Bryant-Denny Stadium are all named in his honor at the University of Alabama.

Well, it was show time for Glen. College can be overwhelming for most mature eighteen-year-olds, registering for classes and figuring out where everything is.

Freshmen are finding their way in an entirely new social setting, one filled with countless parties, clubs, and numerous activities to choose from. Yes, our darling children are going to party some in college, and that's okay. Let's just pray that they manage their activities outside of the classroom enough that it doesn't interfere with their studies.

Instead of attacking Glen verbally when he made mistakes in college, I focused on using a subtle approach. Instead of screaming and yelling, I would speak to him on his level. I would tell him, "When I was your age I struggled with the same issues in college, and because I made poor decisions, these were the adverse consequences that immediately followed!"

I purposely wanted to create a boundary and let Glen know that now he was ultimately responsible for the choices that he made in his life, not me!

Although some of us as parents do try to raise our adult children their whole life, that's impossible and ineffective! When we constantly run and jump through hoops every time, our adult children fall down. It simply means that they will never feel the impact of their mistakes and ensures that we as parents will always have problems!

Children being with their parents should symbolize and be a prerequisite of them inevitably being with God our Father. As parents we should be prepping our children to serve!

There's a substance in us called sin, which is a transgression against God and causes us to commit acts against God! When your adult child understands sin and chooses to fight sin with God's guidance, then we as a parents can claim a victory!

Glen did pretty well his freshman year on and off the football field. There was virtually no home sickness, and he went to his classes. He also maintained a GPA good enough to keep his eligibility so he could play football. To be eligible to play for a division-1 school, you must complete 16 core courses, earn a minimum 2.000 core-course

GPA, and earn a test score that matches your core-course GPA on a sliding scale.

The 2005 recruiting class would feature a stable of running back, consisting of four backs.

Questions and expectations were at their highest margins. Coach Shula and the fans were very excited about the new backs on campus!

Glen was the first one to commit on December 9, 2004, that year. A couple of weeks later the number-one-ranked running back from the state of Florida committed to Bama. Then a week later the second best running back from Florida committed to Bama!

Glen was ranked 3 in the state of Florida. I remember Coach Shula telling me that players commit and de-commit all the time, and I totally understood why.

Shortly after all the running backs had signed, rumors started flying that Glen may de-commit and leave Bama due to the stiff competition. Of course, Glen was interviewed and asked if he was planning on leaving Alabama. He boastfully responded, "I came here to compete against the best! I don't see myself sitting on the bench at all! I'm a very hard worker! I'm coming to start this fall! The one that gets the job done will be the one starting!"

Kenneth Darby was the lone returning veteran running back, and Brodie Croyle was the starting quarterback.

All the rookie backs were very talented. Coach Shula sent a message to all of them stating that "Whoever can block in the back field and pick up the blitz will be on the field!"

With practice getting underway for many teams, one of best luxuries a college football program can have is a state-of-the-art indoor practice facility. Not like in high school were the teams are exposed to the extreme heat or precipitation, these facilities provide shelter and allow teams to get in crucial practices!

While most true freshman across the nation will redshirt and not play their first year, this was not on Glen Coffee's menu. Due to his strong will, competitive drive, and big physical body, he would earn the back-up running back position for the Crimson Tide!

The *Dailey News* wrote a very nice article in the newspaper about how Glen beat out the other backs for playing time. This is speculation on my part, and I don't have any undisputed evidence, but I feel the Fort Walton Beach fans converted from Florida fans to Bama fans overnight due to Glen's efforts on the field.

I was so proud of Glen and couldn't wait to see him on the field in his Bama uniform! Their first game was September 3, 2005, against Middle Tennessee. Glen's number was 38. During Glen's first game, I was sitting in Bryant-Denny with my Bama gear on, which consisted of a hat and jersey. My jersey had number 38 front and back, also our last name, COFFEE, on the back as well.

The game atmosphere was electrifying. Everyone was in a great mode! I didn't realize it at the time, but wearing Glen's jersey number would catch me off guard. As soon as the game started, a lady beside me noticed my jersey and asked me if I was related to Glen. I replied, "Yes, he's my son." Exuberantly, she gave me a big hug and literally thanked me for allowing Glen to play for the Crimson Tide. She even told me that if I needed anything, do not hesitate to ask!

We got into a very engaging conversation about Glen to the point where I wasn't even watching the game! Before I could thank her and get back to the game, to make matters worse, she made an announcement to all the surrounding fans that I was Glen's dad!

I was immediately bombarded with so many questions that it became somewhat overwhelming, and I literally started looking for an escape route! At that time I remembered my coworkers asking me if I had ever been to an Alabama football game. They were trying to prepare me. They did tell me that Alabama fans have a winning history like no other and that they are the most committed, loyal, supportive fans in college football!

After everyone settled down, we started watching the game, screaming, yelling, acting crazy, and just having a ball. It was so much fun!

I watched my son make history for our family by playing in his first college football game. And by the way I didn't wear any Bama apparel at the next game!

Glen won his first college game. The score was 26–7. I averaged around six games per season when Glen was playing for Alabama. The next game I attended was October 1 against the Florida Gators! Bryant-Denny Stadium was bursting at the seams with over 82,000 spectators there!

I had to park in the midst of Gator fans due to unavailability of parking. Some fans just came to tailgate. There were parties everywhere, just a fun-filled day.

Glen had a spectacular game. Afterwards, I stayed a chatted with him for a while before I headed back to Florida.

I would take Highway 82 east then 65 south to get home. I had missed most of the traffic, so I was on 82 east driving home and I passed a policeman going westbound. The speed limit was fifty-five miles per hour. I immediately glanced at my speedometer, and I was going around sixty-two miles per hour.

I reduced my speed back to fifty-five and periodically watched the police car until it almost disappeared in my rearview mirror. Then right at the last minute the policeman turned around, heading my way! I was thinking, *I know he's not after me because I'm not speeding!* So he gets directly behind me and inevitably puts his lights on and pulls me over!

At this point I was slightly irritated! The policeman got out of his car and walks to my car. Before I could say anything, the officer said, "Okay, you're wearing an Alabama hat and you have Florida tags!"

I replied, "Yes, sir, my son plays for Alabama."

The officer replied abruptly in disbelief, "Sir, I need to see your driver license."

I gave him my license, and he looked at it and smiled.

Surprisingly, he said with excitement, "GLEN COFFEE! Glen is your son?"

I said "Yes, sir."

The officer said, "Mr. Coffee, I know Glen very well. Matter of fact I know all the Bama football players!"

Then we started elaborating about the game! The officer told me that he was on the sideline working security for the game. About twenty minutes later, the officer told me that Glen was a very respectable young man! He sent me on my way by saying, "Have a great ride home, and I'll see you next game, Mr. Coffee. ROLL TIDE!"

Glen played in all twelve games his freshman year. He rushed for a season-high seventy-five yards in their win against South Carolina.

Glen had a total of 179 yards on 48 attempts and caught eight passes for 91 yards, including 1 touchdown!

Freshman year... Absolutely nothing went as planned. Girls galore nope. Freshman all American, nope. ESPN highlights, nope. It's funny to look back but as an incoming freshman you fail to realize that because anything is possible, anything also can mean performing horribly. At the time, however failure wasn't an option and my plans for glory were just about to be underway, or so I thought. That 2005 running back commit class included the number 1(Mike Ford) and 2(Roy Upchurch) ranked rb's in the state of Florida. I and another position mate, Ali Shariff, rounded out the bunch. FYI, I was ranked 4th. As dad said, competition didn't bother me, somehow some way I'd find a place to start. I received a little help from Mike as he ended up being un-eligible due to grades. Admittedly relief was my first reaction, dude was a beast. Summer of my freshman year went exactly as planned. A simple plan it was. In summer workouts, outwork not only the in-coming running backs but every other incoming freshman.

CHAPTER 7

Glen Finds Christ at Bama

Glen's freshman football season was over. It had substance, and he definitely laid a good foundation to build from. During the off-season, most coaches around the country would give their players a break from meetings, practice, and film study that occurred throughout the active football season.

Coaches realize that it's crucial for a student-athlete to have time to study for exams.

All players aren't just turned loose for the semester. Most head coaches will have mandatory study hall hours so the players can meet with their tutors.

Glen had managed his GPA well and did come home for a brief moment. It was a blessing seeing him grow into a young man. He also clearly understood that he had to raise his expectations and put a demand on his life and keep reaching for the NFL.

Recovering from injuries are every football player's number one priority during the off- season. Glen had a groin injury. True reality of a football player is, if you're on the field playing, you are always injured in some form or fashion.

Being a college football player is a life where you are constantly evaluating your performance. Speed and agility are always on players' priority list. Glen knew he had to stay ahead of the game by staying at the practice facility during off-season.

His goal was to train his muscles to fire in a specific sequence, and program his body to hold the patterns. Then he would be successful in developing speed and decrease injury potentially at the same time.

The A-Day game is an annual college football exhibition game set at the conclusion of spring practice by the University of Alabama Crimson Tide.

The game is normally played around mid-April, so all the players are back at school now practicing. One thing for sure playing for the Crimson Tide is that your position is never guaranteed. You are always battling for playing time.

With Kenneth Darby preparing to leave for the NFL, the starting running back position was up for grabs and things were definitely within an arm's reach for Glen.

If things go the way they're supposed to go, Glen would be the starting back that season. But not only will he be competing against his recruiting class, Coach Shula has added two more running back to the 2006 recruiting class.

There are countless differences between high school and college football. In high school football it's uncommon and practically unheard of for a freshman to come in and take a junior or senior's starting position. In college football, the coaches only want to know one thing— who's the best player for that particular position to help us win!

I arrived at Bryant-Denny Stadium April 1, 2006, for the A-Day game and the attendance was over forty thousand fans. WOW!

Glen didn't play due to a groin injury that was later diagnosed as a sports hernia. He would undergo surgery with no complications, thankfully! Due to a very successful operation, Glen's doctor predicted that he would be ready for fall practice.

Summer passed and the forever dreaded fall camp was fast approaching. Roy Upchurch, who from the start became a brother, would be my stiffest competition for second string. Kenneth Darby had the starting job on lockdown, and anyway I'd already surmised freshman All-American possibilities with KD being the pseudo starter. Two goals, I knew, needed to be accomplished to beat Roy out. With only a month of camp and the perceived notion his talent trumped mine, I avoided a head to head battle of skill. The check list included making fewer mistakes than him and showing I was the better pass blocker. Avid reader, photographic memory, play book, blitz pick up.

Fall practice started with Glen wearing a black practice jersey, which signifies no hitting to avoid further injury. Glen's status was upgraded to full contact the third week of fall practice. During a Monday evening scrimmage, he would suffer a knee injury that would sideline him his whole sophomore season. The impact of the hit was so horrific that it rendered him motionless. The entire practice session paused, hoping Glen would get up on his own, but he had to be escorted off the field by the medical staff.

This setback, like no other, would affect Glen physically and mentally. Prior to the injury Glen was in contention for significant playing time as the reserve back! Hopefully infrequent, but injuries are an unavoidable part of sports.

Can you imagine how this setback could deplete an elite athlete's soul? Glen's status went from backup running back for the most decorated college football program in the world to virtually nonexistent.

Life really gets exciting when a person starts to figure out their true purpose in life.

However, for some student-athletes, the psychological response to injury can trigger or unmask serious mental health issues such as depression, anxiety, substances abuse, sadness, lake of motivation, and anger.

These are the characteristics of the fruits of the spirit: love, joy, peace, long-suffering, kindness, goodness, faithfulness, gentleness, and self-control. The unpopular one that stands out and seems out of place is long-suffering.

In the Bible, the apostle Paul reminds us that the sufferings of this present time are not worthy to be compared with the glory which shall be revealed to us (Rom. 8:18).

Suffering enhances our ability to pray under the burden of suffering; however, one will learn to pray as he never has prayed before.

The Alabama coaching staff decided it was best to medically redshirt Glen due to his injury. The redshirt meant that Glen would be withdrawn from football for one year in order to develop skills and extend the period of playing eligibility by a further year.

Redshirt players are still required to go to class, make all teams meetings, and complete all therapy.

Glen was devastated and went into a form of depression. He had put all his eggs in one basket; and football was his life, passion, his everything. So he began to mope around campus and the classroom! Attempting to seek some comfort in his shattered world, Glen visited his close teammate Roy Upchurch. Roy, another running back, was recovering from an injury. He was depressed and redshirted as well!

So they both would sit around miserable, asking the question, "Why did this happen to me?"

Before their injuries occurred, they would hang out daydreaming and brainstorming about how they were going to make All-SEC and inevitably make it to the NFL.

To make matters worse, Glen and Roy would leave class early or sometimes just skip all together. This pattern quickly got them both in the *dog house*, a term used when players get on the coaches black list. Coach Burns was their running back coach. One day at a team meeting, he made an announcement, "Glen, Roy, I've got this list and your names are on it. Can you stay after the meeting, please?"

Coach Burns clearly understood their crisis and simply wanted to help them get their identity back. Therefore, he wasted no time by getting in their faces and telling them, "You got to snap out of this depressed state! The injury is only temporary! The crimson jersey that you're wearing, do you really understand how privileged and blessed you are?"

Coach Burns lecture helped, but their egos were still crushed! When we have problems in our life God wants us to turn to him for answers, not this world. Also, when God has chosen you to perform a task, He will test your faith to see how you measure up. When hard times happen, the true nature of our faith will be revealed.

God doesn't test us because he doesn't know how strong we are. Instead he tests us because we don't know how strong we are and we'll only realize it when times of testing come.

Testing should make us spiritually stronger. In the Book of Genesis God promised a son through Sarah who was barren at the time and Abraham who was impotent as well. Supernaturally, God blessed them both and established His everlasting covenant with Isaac and his seed (Gen. 17:19–21). Later on, after Isaac is born and a young boy, God commands Abraham to take him to the land of Moriah and slay him for a burnt offering! Truly God was testing Abraham's faith! Abraham, being a faithful servant, rose up the next morning and gathered everything that he needed for the burnt offering, including Isaac and two male servants (Gen. 22:23). As they approached Mount Moriah, Abraham instructed his male servants to wait there while he and Isaac went up to worship, ensuring that they both would return afterwards. Abraham loved, respected, and feared God with all his heart and did exactly what God had instructed him to do. As he raised his hand with the knife to slay his son, an angel of the Lord shouted, "Abraham, Abraham, lay not thine hand upon the lad, neither do thou anything unto him!" God spared Isaac because Abraham truly loved Him first!

Throughout the Holy Bible our ancestors are constantly demonstrating the type of faith that God expects from us, but the reality is that we're still wandering in the wilderness.

Since Glen was redshirted, he had more time to focus on his classwork. One day he returned home from class and discovered that he had a new roommate. His name was Matt Watson. Glen didn't know it at the time, but Matt would become one of the most influential persons in his life. He would also trigger one of the biggest turning points in Glen's career.

Matt was a gifted track star and had earned a student-athlete scholarship as well. Some of the things that Glen noticed about Matt immediately was that he was quiet, very polite, always in a good mood, and he always had a Bible with him. Matt was so different compared to the other students that Glen became curious. There was a quality about Matt that Glen envied. So one day Glen asked Matt, "Hey, bro, why do you carry a Bible with you everywhere you go?" Matt replied, "I carry my Bible because I believe that our Lord and Savior Jesus Christ died for our sins!"

So step by step, day by day, Matt would break down the Bible verses to Glen; and he started to develop a love for God's Living Word.

The void and emptiness that had occupied Glen's heart was being filled with the Holy Spirit. True Christians don't have to make countless announcements and tell the world that they're a Christian, they lead by example.

In the Book of James, Jesus's brother James was bothered by his observation that Christians were not living holy and righteous lives, too many of them failed to show any difference in their behavior after becoming believers. So James insisted vigorously that faith by itself, if it is not accompanied by action, is dead.

Even in our modern world today, some Christians go to church because it's routine or a family tradition. When they read God's word, they give their opinion instead of submitting!

God does not need nor is he concerned about our sinful opinions. We should pray that the world sees the God in us first, not us.

Is our love for God a fraudulent love? True love never quits, gives up, or takes a day off!

CHAPTER 8

The Cover of Sports Illustrated

Glen had a new purpose in life now. Amazingly, football was no longer his number one priority in life. He took his Bible with him everywhere he went. He had a relentless pursuit and was gravitating toward God with every heart beat that he took.

He was doing a lot better in school. His knee injury was healing well, and he just didn't stress out about things.

Finding Christ had put everything into perspective for Glen. Terry Grant, a true freshman, along with senior running back Kenneth Darby, carried the load while Glen was out during his sophomore year.

Glen returned to the 2007 Alabama Crimson Tide team under new head coach Nick Saban. Coach Saban would turn out to be one the greatest coaches that Glen had ever experienced. Coach Saban mastered the ability to identify and bring out talent in players that they never knew exist! He also understood that each athlete on their team was different in attitude, personality, responsibility, sensitivity, and how they handle criticism and adversity.

Glen would start his 2007 season with a new coach and new outlook on life. He had surrendered his life to Christ and felt a true sense of love and happiness. He had rededicated himself to football by putting Christ first.

With Christ there's no quitting. Glen knew that Christ had his back, regardless of the number of touchdowns that he scored. Every touchdown that he scored would be for Christ! During an interview, Glen told a reporter that every touchdown that he scored would be for Christ. He also said, "Football is my ministry now, and I used it to glorify God. If anyone tries to tackle me, that means they're trying to stop me from giving glory to God, and I'm not having that!"

Glen vowed to God that "every second that he breathe, every minute that he lived," he was doing so in the name of Jesus. "During the bad and the good, I have to glorify Jesus and call His name!"

As Christians we must strive to hold each other accountable in every area of our lives.

The Crimson Tide would host Western Carolina in the 2007 opening game. Glen rushed 9 times for 76 yards and 1 touchdown in a 52–6 victory. He had his first 100-yard rushing game in their season homecoming and landed a 30–24 victory over Houston.

Glen finished the season with 545 yards on 129 carries, scoring 4 touchdowns. He also caught passes for 142 yards.

He was baptized at a local church in Tuscaloosa. He had a fresh haircut and shave prior to his baptism. Seeing him on fire for Christ was such a precious moment in my life.

This is what God says in 1 John 2:15–16. Don't love the world's ways. Don't love the world's goods. Love of the world squeezes out the love for the Father. Practically everything that goes on in the world—wanting your own way, wanting everything for yourself, wanting to appear important—has nothing to do with the Father. It just isolates you from Him!

Prior to starting the 2008 season, Glen received an Off-the-Field Community Service Award. The award ceremony was held at the chapel on campus. Coach Saban intentionally wanted the players to witness the importance of the award by marching the whole team into the church. During Glen's acceptance speech, he commented on the sudden death of Mr. Bernie Mac, the entertainer. Glen said, "Mr. Bernie Mac has passed, and I don't know his relationship with God, but if I die today, I know in my heart that I will have eternal life with my Father in heaven."

Glen was also a member of the FCA, Fellowship of Christian Athletes. The mission of the FCA is to present to coaches and athletes, and all whom they influence, the challenge and adventure of receiving Jesus Christ as Savior and Lord, serving Him in their relationship and in the fellowship of the church.

As the 2008 fall practice hit full bloom, the talk on campus was that the Crimson Tide wanted to adopt a different running style. The coaching staff wanted a big back with a pounding running style to run the ball downhill!

Due to Glen's determination and power running style, he was the main candidate for the position. Once again, Glen would start the season with a minor injury! He would have a minor tear repaired in his shoulder and wouldn't participate in the A-Day game. However, he would be ready for August practice.

Glen was name the starter in all fourteen games due to a dominating August practice.

The Crimson Tide would face the Clemson Tigers August 30 in the Inaugural Chick-Fil-A College Kickoff. The game was played at a neutral location in the Georgia Dome in Atlanta. The ninth ranked Clemson Tigers were favored to win over the twenty-fourth ranked Crimson Tide.

Expectations were extremely high for the Clemson fans after hearing all summer long how loaded they were in every skilled position. The Clemson coaching staff felt the odds where in their favor to win their first Atlantic Coast Conference (ACC) football title in seventeen years.

Coach Burton Burns, Bama's running back coach, was the hidden force behind Alabama's dominating ground game.

After adopting a smashmouth, power-running style, the Crimson Tide would catch all opposition off guard and deliver a punishing attack.

Some sports analysts say that Glen's power-run style brought the swagger back to Bama. Glen took the field and pounded the Clemson defensive line with unshakable, decisive moves and always fell forward for a couple of extra yards after contact. When he got tired, back-up running back Mark Ingram would come in with the same mind-set and deliver another damaging blow.

The Alabama ground attack proved to be lethal, and the Clemson coaching staff stood speechless on the sideline. The Alabama defense had a stout performance as well by shutting down Clemson's James Davis and C. J. Spiller, the duo known as Thunder and Lightning. They both only combined for only 20 yards on the ground, compared to the Alabama backs that combined for a total of 263 yards.

With ESPN's college game-day crew in town and Clemson selected as preseason favorites, the Crimson Tide would upset the Tigers 34–10 to open the season.

Glen finished the game with 97 yards. The play-by-play TV announcers were Brent Musburger and Kirk Herbstreit. Their post-game comments were "Is Bama back?"

Alabama's dominating performance helped propel them from No. 24 to No. 13 in the polls. The national media took notice, and *Sports Illustrated* awarded Glen by featuring him on the cover of their world-renowned magazine. The photo was an illustration of Glen plowing through the Clemson defensive line with two defenders latched onto him.

The headline of the magazine read: "SEC Beware: Alabama sends an early warning!" Glen's comments were, "Coach Saban has been working us very hard, and we've bought into his coaching scheme" and "We're the best team in college football now. We expect other teams to fear us!"

A new spirit had been re-awakened in Glen, and that spirit was Christ! At an early age, he had unmasked the mysteries of life. The only thing a person needs to do is find out who Jesus Christ is and read the blueprint of life, the Bible!

Glen had found Christ, and Christ had found him!

CHAPTER 9

The Blow Out

In Glen's spiritual growth, his main objective was to glorify and gravitate toward Jesus Christ. In every game he came out fired up for Jesus and gave his best performance.

All Americans are physically free, but if our spirit hasn't been born again, we are surely bound by sin. In John 3:6 Jesus puts it this way: "That which is born of flesh is flesh, and that which is born of the spirit is spirit." Therefore, Jesus insists that we must be born again. To underline the serious bondage that we are in prior to our spiritual birth, Paul says this in Romans: "The mind that is set on the flesh is hostile to God, for it does not submit to God's law." Indeed, it cannot.

By now everyone has noticed the remarkable change in Glen's personality, especially his teammates! There were mixed vibes, and that's okay. One of Glen's teammates commented on his Bible in the practice facility by saying, "You have your Bible here? Man, you're faking!" Glen responded, "It is what it is. I'll pray that someday your eyes will be open as mine were."

On the other hand, six-foot-four, 325-pound left tackle Andre Smith praised Glen for his leadership on and off the field. As fans, we are entertained on Saturdays by watching our favorite players perform, but we don't get a chance to witness their incredible work ethic in the weight room.

Andre immediately became a fan of Glen's when he witnessed his Hulk-like performance handling the weights. Andre shared with a local reporter, Mr. Ian Rapoport, that Glen was the second strongest player on the team, with an exception of one of the nose tackles. Andre also told Mr. Rapoport that Glen was just a freakish athlete. "He's even stronger than me in some cases!" He set several high school weight-lifting records in Florida!

This new discovery about Glen was so intriguing that the reporter decided to dig deeper by asking Andre to elaborate about Glen's off-the-field life. Andre responded by saying, "He's a great guy. On and off the field, he's a great guy. Big-time Christian! Glen does FCA every Monday, and you can count on him doing something that involves Christ every day!"

After a lengthy interview and gathering pages of notes, Mr. Rapoport felt compelled to find the origin of Glen's eminence by contacting his high school coach, Mike Owens. Coach Owens eagerly described Glen as a selfless, workout-warrior type guy, with an elite work ethic. Coach Owens added, "In the state of Florida, we have a state weight-lifting competition, which is a combination of power lifting and Olympic style. Glen walked away with it his senior year, and it wasn't even close. By the way, to set the record straight, his senior year stats were stunning: benching 390, cleaning 365, and squatting 500 pounds."

Of course, my favorite SEC stadium is Bryant-Denny in Tuscaloosa, Alabama, but they're all state of the art, elaborate structures. For example, Neyland Stadium home of the Tennessee Volunteers has a capacity of 102,455 people. Can you imagine being in the midst of one hundred thousand savvy, screaming fans. That type of environment generates so much continuity that it makes one feel that they can produce their own electromagnetic field. Don't mention tailgate heaven, where you're constantly being enticed with the aroma of brats, barbeque ribs, chicken, potato salad, etc., and a sea of parties.

In September 20, 2008, the Arkansas Razorbacks would host the Crimson Tide at the beautiful Donald W. Reynolds Stadium located in Fayetteville, Arkansas. Fayetteville sets at an elevation of 1,400 feet, with its foundation carved into the Ozark Mountains. Their natural beauty creates a stunning postcard setting.

This victory for Glen will truly be one of the most memorable of his career. He would have a career day and unleash his fury on the Razorbacks by scoring 2 touchdowns and accumulated 162 yards. He was truly a force to be reckoned with! This display of excellence would award Glen with his first 100-yard rushing performance that season. It also birth his career-long run of 87 yards, which at that time was the longest in the SEC.

The Razorbacks would put together a solid drive, but the stout Alabama defense would hold them at their one-yard line to close out the half with Bama up 35–7.

Arkansas received the second half kickoff, but Alabama would intercept the ball on the first play of the second half.

Glen received a handoff from John Parker Wilson, Bama's quarterback, then he exploded though another gaping hole created by the offensive line and waltz into the end zone with a thirty-one-yard touchdown.

The bond between running backs and offensive linemen is like no other. If everything goes perfect between the running back and the offensive linemen, the two will never touch. When they create an opening, the back has to hit it hard and not look back.

Most tailbacks will applaud their offensive line by admitting that without them, they're ineffective.

The Crimson Tide would have their way against the Razorbacks. The final score was 49–14. The 49 points scored were the most points scored by Alabama in an SEC game since a 59–28 victory over Vanderbilt in 1990.

At this point Glen was on every college coach's radar, and the media had put him under a microscope.

God empowered Glen and put him in the middle of one of the biggest platforms in college football for a reason. In Luke 22:32 God says, "But I have prayed for thee, that thy faith fail not: and when thou art converted, strengthen thy brethren."

When God blesses us with a gift, he wants us to share it, not contain it. God uses us to demonstrate His power in us to show the world that He is "I AM!"

The next showdown I would attend would be Alabama vs. Georgia, September 27. The game was showcased at beautiful Sanford Stadium in Athens, Georgia. Ranked no. 8, the Crimson Tide would come in as the underdogs against the no. 3 ranked Georgia Bulldogs. A win for the Dawgs could possibly give them a no. 1 ranking.

You can imagine the hype that had been brewing for these to powerhouses!

For whatever reason, the Georgia coaching staff decided that their players and fans would wear black jerseys to create a black-out atmosphere. Even today this 2008 cross-divisional showdown between the Crimson Tide and the Dawgs is known as the Blackout!

The attendance for the game was 92,746. I would say at least 90,000 fans had donned their black tops. The Georgia fans were loud, rowdy, disorderly, and very vocal. They could smell a win and openly boasted about how they were going to kick Bama's "you know what!"

It was definitely a climate of ire and borderline hostility as well. One thing that stood out—policemen were everywhere. I really didn't know if that was a good or bad sign.

Anticipation was peaking, Bama fans were taunting the Dawg fans by saying, "The reason you're wearing black is because you're going to attend a funeral tonight!" I was hoping that our Bama fans would tone it down some because we were totally outnumbered!

The roar from the stadium was so loud I could feel my inner organs vibrating. It was a madhouse!

The game starts and the Dawgs win the toss and defer the ball to the Tide. Big mistake! Bama would drive the ball seventy-three yards and inevitably punch it in for a touchdown. Bama would use all three running backs to pound on the Georgia defense, a relentless pursuit in Alabama fashion.

Bama's defense was stifling, and their offense was dominating. They would close the first half, tide up 30–0!

The Georgia fans were shocked, speechless, the rage shown on their faces. I could see policemen breaking up Dawg fights throughout the stadium!

This was just a clean old-fashioned hateful game! Glen would score his first touchdown in the first half. In the second half, Georgia's offense would move the ball down the field, but had to settle for a thirty-three-yard field goal.

The Dawgs attempted a comeback, but the Alabama defense was just too stout. Bama would wake up midway through the fourth quarter by scoring more points to extend the lead.

Glen would give Alabama a good burst of fresh air by scoring his second touchdown of the game on a twelve-yard run. The final score of the game would be 41–30, Bama!

Alabama, with its stout defense, dominated Georgia on the line of scrimmage, pounded them with the running game, and negated their run attempts. Glen finished the game with two touchdowns on eighty-seven yards rushing.

The leaders for the Crimson Tide really stood up for the game. Coach Mark Richt, head coach for the Georgia Bulldogs, told the media that "the Glen Coffee that showed up tonight is definitely not the same Coffee that we played last year!"

I was very happy for the big W for the Tide and hoping that I would depart the stadium without a confrontation. As I stated before we were surely outnumbered and in deep MAD DAWG COUNTRY!

And wouldn't you know it, to add fuel to the fire, the Bama fans started singing our victory song, "Hey Georgia! Hey Georgia! Hey Georgia! We just beat the hell outta you! Rammer Jammer Yellow Hammer Give 'em hell, Alabama!"

At that point the field was covered with debris. Objects were flying everywhere! The policemen really earned their pay that night to say the least!

The Crimson Tide would face the Kentucky Wildcats October 4, ranked no. 2 in the nation. It would be their highest ranking in fifteen years.

Glen would rush for a season-high 218 yards, including a touchdown. The 218 yards gained by Glen were the most by a Crimson Tide running back since Shaun Alexander in 1996.

Of course, Glen loved playing for the University of Alabama and supporting his teammates. He also purposely enjoyed talking to reporters after the game as well to give honor to God!

Most reporters wanted to know the secret to his success and his miraculous transformation that year. In response, Glen would let it flow, "Jesus, Jesus, Jesus, Jesus, and Jesus!" He shared with one reporter: "We can often miss or misunderstand the real passion with which some people truly run after Jesus. For them, Jesus becomes their everything, and everything else becomes secondary! In other words, when I'm out there on the field running, I'm also running for Jesus to give him the glory!"

I felt so blessed to see my son standing for Christ! It was also neat to witness his uncanny ability to anticipate the opposition, wait for his blockers, then explode down the field. Glen continued running for Christ all season long, creating one of the most impressive resumes in college football.

When you say the word *rivalry*, what two universities define it better than Alabama and Auburn football.

This iconic game was once played in Birmingham, Alabama, for many years. The term *Iron Bowl* originates from Birmingham's rich historic role in the steel industry.

Alabama would host Auburn November 29 with the no. 1 ranking at Bryant-Denny Stadium. The game truly was and always will be the most anticipated game between the two football giants!

Glen's former high school running back coach was an avid Bama fan, so I met him at his tailgating site at Bryant-Denny prior to the game!

Another highlight for me was that two of my brothers came out of town to support Glen as well. We were all there celebrating, partying, and just grateful for the Crimson Tide and Glen's breakthrough season. The moment was so surreal!

Glen's last regular game of the season would be nothing short of a heroic Hollywood ending! Glen would rush for 144 yards and 1 touchdown contributing to a 36–0 victory over the Auburn Tigers.

This statement win ended a six-year drought were Auburn had dominated the rivalry. Glen landed a dagger in the Auburn defense by breaking for a forty-one-yard touchdown! After the touchdown, in order to stimulate the fans even further, he continued running down the sideline in a victory dance, beating his chest vigorously chanting, "LET'S GO, LET'S GO, and LET'S GO!"

The trademark snapshot of Glen running between center Antione Caldwell and left tackle Andre Smith became a masterpiece that night. Their efforts were so revealing that it inspired internationally-acclaimed sports artist Daniel A. Moore to create Glen's famous portrait, *THE BLOW OUT*!

It was Coach Saban's first victory in the rivalry! He even admitted that he was doing a post-game victory dance in the locker room.

The headlines for the next day *Tuscaloosa News* Sunday sports page read, "COFFEE RUNS OVER AUBURN!"

CHAPTER 10

Glen Enters the NFL Draft

The SEC Championship game matches up the Eastern and Western divisions of the Southeastern Conference. The SEC Conference was also the first conference to host a championship game.

The Crimson Tide, Western representatives, would face the Florida Gators, Eastern representatives, in the 2008 Dr. Pepper SEC Championship. The game was played December 6 in the Georgia Dome in Atlanta.

This game was easily one of the most anticipated games of the year for Bama Nation and the Florida Gators. Whoever would win this game would surely play for the BCS National Championship.

To add even more popularity to this game, the no. 1 ranked Crimson Tide facing the no. 2 ranked Florida Gators would be the first of its kind in NCAA history!

Glen would have a spectacular game by scoring the first touchdown for the Crimson Tide on an 18-yard run. With his smash mouth run style, he also rushed for 112 yards on 21 carries. Despite the heroic effort from Glen and his teammates, Tim Tebow and the Florida Gators would hand them their first loss of the year! The final score was 31–20, Gators!

The Crimson Tide was awarded the very popular All-State Sugar Bowl in New Orleans, Louisiana. The game would be played at the Super Dome. On January 2, 2009, the no. 4 Crimson Tide would face off with the no. 6 Utah Utes. Unfortunately, the Utes would shock Bama Nation by pulling off an upset over the heavily favored Crimson Tide! The final score was 31–17, Utes!

Glen finished his 2008 season owning the two longest runs in the Southeastern Conference. He led his team rushing with 233 attempts for 1,383 yards and 10 touchdowns!

In some cases, the running back is the best athlete on the team. At any given time, he may receive a hand off out of the back field, or receive a pass, or pass block picking up the blitz, he may even be required to throw the ball in some occasions.

Glen received two conference awards. He was named to the AP ALL-SEC First Team and the Coaches ALL-SEC Second Team.

The Crimson Tide would hold their annual awards banquet at the elegant Wynfrey Hotel in Birmingham, Alabama.

Coach Saban applauded the team by telling them how proud he was for their accomplishments. He also elaborated on how difficult it is to go 12–0 in a real BCS conference. Coach Saban awarded Glen with the team's Most Valuable Player award after posting the fourth-highest single-season rushing total (1,347) in school history!

As we waited to be served at our tables, I noticed the attire of the waiters. They all wore tuxedoes and white gloves. They also stood behind us waiting to serve our food. As the food came out, they served us individually with one arm folded behind their backs.

"How impressive!" I was truly honored with their royal service and Southern hospitality.

Of course, the food was magnificent, but how could I not pinch myself to make sure I wasn't dreaming. I was eating dinner with Nick Saban, Coach Burns, Glen Coffee, Andre Smith, Julio Jones, Mark Ingram, just to name a few! They all were overachievers! I was in the midst of some of the greatest athletes in the world. They all would graduate and some worked on their graduate degree!

The world needs godly leaders! Imagine if you could do an internship with this elite group for a year or so. You think the exposure would enhance your game of life? "Iron sharpens iron!"

Underline this next statement: if you are around lazy, bitter, negative, abusive people all your life, it becomes your norm! We are attracted to what we are exposed to. It becomes our norm, an oxymoron!

At some point in our lives, we all will experience this world of true lies!

In Genesis 12:1 God told Abraham, "Leave your country, your family and your father's home for a land that I will show you. I'll make you a great nation and bless you."

When God called Abraham, he was in the city of Babylonia. Babylonia was a modern city, having libraries, schools, and a system of law. Abraham's father, Terah, worshiped idols. He was referred to as the idol maker. Babylonia was an evil, sinful city that worshipped many different Gods, such as the God of fire, moon, sun, and stars.

Every female in the city at some point in her life would have to take her turn in serving as a priestess harlot in the temple.

With a father who worshipped idols and a city dedicated to wickedness, Abraham was not raised in the best environment. Yet, when God called Abraham, he believed God and by faith followed Gods instructions!

Abraham left his home not even knowing where he was going!

With a very productive junior season behind him, Glen decided to forego his senior year and declare the NFL Draft!

Even at this point in Glen's life, God was telling him to finish college and follow Him!

Even though football was no longer Glen's main love anymore, he had convinced himself to leave school early and enter the NFL!

Due to the close bond that he had with his teammates, Glen decided to share his plans of leaving for the NFL to some of them. The news of Glen's potential departure quickly spread throughout campus.

Finally, Coach Saban got wind of the rumor and quickly arranged a meeting with Glen. They would meet three times prior to Glen making his final decision.

In the first meeting Coach Saban was very calm, not a lot of eye contact. Coach Saban started the meeting by saying, "Tell me about the rumor that I'm hearing about you declaring the NFL Draft."

Glen responds, "Yes, I think I'm ready."

Coach Saban says, "First, I don't think you're ready. You need to play your senior year, but I will contact the draft board to see what round you're projected to go."

In the second meeting, still not a lot of eye contact, Coach Saban informed Glen that the board has projected him to go fifth or sixth round. Glen responded by saying, "That's fine. I just need to get my foot in the door, and I'll do the rest."

Coach Saban strongly disagreed and told him, "You need to play your senior year to get a higher draft pick!"

In the third meeting, Coach Saban was looking directly at Glen and he was livid and immediately let him know how he felt in Coach-Saban fashion!

Glen had made his mind up and announced January 9, 2009, that he would forgo his senior year and declare for the NFL Draft. His representing agent would be Todd Crannell of Q2 Sports & Entertainment.

As his dad, I have to admit I was stoked to hear that he would enter the NFL Draft. In relation to him leaving school early, yes, there was a question mark on my part. I understood that my parenting days in the flesh were over. It was time for me to be a praying parent and pray for Glen and trust God to do the things that I could not do.

This was a statement that Glen released to the media:

> I really enjoyed my time at the University of Alabama, but I think it's the right time for me to move on to the NFL. Alabama has been a tremendous place for me to develop as both a football player and a person. I couldn't have asked for a better group of coaches. I want to personally thank Coach (Nick) Saban and Coach (Burton) Burns for everything they have done for me!

Of course, Coach Saban is world renowned for winning championships. He could probably run for the presidency and easily win. One area in his life where he doesn't get enough recognition is for his uncanny ability to mentor and in some cases be a positive father figure to his players.

Glen would train for the 2009 NFL Combine at the luxurious Perdido Key Sportsplex in Pensacola, Florida, only forty minutes from his home in Fort Walton Beach, Florida.

Most of the players competing for the combine would arrive at their training facility in the first week in January.

Glen would spend the next six weeks or so training for the biggest job interview in his life.

Although Glen wasn't a professional football player at this point of his career, this is when he started to taste the lavish lifestyle of the rich and famous! Combined with speaking engagements and endorsements, Glen had earned a whopping $75,000 prior to even turning pro!

Glen's goal at the training facility was simply to become bigger, faster, and stronger!

This was a typical training day at the Sportsplex:

8:00 a.m. – wake up

8:30 a.m. – breakfast

9:00 a.m. – team meeting or daily objectives.

9:45 a.m. – workout 1 (on the field for combine specific drill, including vertical jump, forty-yard dash and agility and position drills)

11:30 a.m. – lunch

2:15 p.m. – workout 2 (in the weight room to train plyometric, Olympic lifts, lower and upper body)

4:00 p.m. – recovery and regeneration session including hot tube, ice tube, chiropractic adjustments, massage, post-workout, and supplementation.

5:30 p.m. – dinner

7:00 p.m. – team focused on interviewing skills.

The sports nutritionist would carefully plan out each meal, and the position coaches would assist the athletes in preparing for the position-specific drills that will be conducted on the field in Indianapolis.

The combine tryouts are definitely an epic event. The best elite athletes in the world are showcasing their gladiator-like skills for the whole world to view.

Glen arrived in Indianapolis February 18, 2009, for his NFL Combine debut. Lucas Oil Stadium has hosted this profound contest year after year.

The evaluation process for the draft creates an atmosphere of a Hollywood movie shoot. The sidelines are embedded with tons of video equipment and dominated by NFL owners, scouts, players, and reporters.

The prospects on the field have fire in their eyes and poses the heart of a lion on the hunt! This is the arena where great athletes are breed!

Mental toughness is the capacity to reliable perform at your best, regardless of external conditions, distractions, or internal emotions.

Glen would dazzle the evaluation board by putting up top performer numbers, causing his draft stock to climb even higher. The combine staff had Glen listed at 6 feet 210 pounds. His well-built frame would give him top performer honors.

He ran his 40-yard dash in 4.5 seconds, vertical leap was 36 inches, bench press 225 pounds 24 times, and his shuttle speed was 4.51. Another attribute that helped Glen's draft stock was his speaking ability. He was a sought-after speaker in the community and thrived to share his faith with the world.

The 2009 NFL Draft would take place at Radio City Music Hall in New York City on April 25 and 26.

Now the participants of the combine would have to play a "hurry up and wait" game, hoping to hear any insight where their draft number may land.

Glen did manage to get a call from a sports reporter. He informed Glen that his stock was indeed rising, instead of a fifth or sixth pick, he could potentially go late second round or early third! WOW, that was a good jump! It wasn't written in stone, just pure speculation, but it sure did sound good!

Glen was drafted in the third round of the 2009 NFL with the seventy-fourth overall pick by the San Francisco 49ers. Praise God!

It was the celebration of the universe! We all were so happy for Glen and his achievements!

He had ran the race of life and made it to one of its finish lines! To put everything in perspective, I was just happy that he had a job!

In the midst of the celebrating, his whole life journey unfolded in my mind, as though I was watching it on a big screen TV. The vision took me way back when Glen was playing pick-up football in the streets of Saudi Arabia, a little boy with a dream and a passion for a sport. Then middle school, high school, and at one point in college, things got rough for Glen and we didn't know if he was going to make it to the finish line! But God had a plan for him!

There are no straight paths to God. He will purposely set a booby trap in your life to test your faith! When the war starts, the commander only wants to know two things—who's going to run and who's going to stay and fight!

God will measure our faith as we stand at the door of adversity! Glen was a praying soldier, and God saw the fight in him!

As Christians we need to find our purpose of service. We have lost the art of serving, but we need to remember that we are responsible for the next generation.

Why should we expect our youth to stay in church when we don't?

We would soon discover that God was indeed preparing Glen for the next challenge in his life.

CHAPTER 11

Rookie Year with the 49ers

Twenty-two-year-old Glen Coffee Jr. would sign a four-year contract with the 49ers valued at 2.578 million dollars. Topped off with a signing bonus of $828,000 dollars!

I would say that's a decent first job starting salary if you ask me! We all think that we want to be rich and famous, and it's nothing wrong with having money. We couldn't survive in this modern-day world without it.

God talks very openly about how he wants us to have an abundant lifestyle. People that have gained wealth legally have paid the price buy sacrificing their life and countless hours in some form or fashion.

God also talks very openly about the lust of money and how dangerous it is when it's used out of context.

Some friends and family were genuinely sincere about Glen's success. We would soon find out that others had hidden agendas! Even before Glen had left for the 49er's minicamp, I noticed some people were literally trapping him in the corner with their shopping list! Some just expected him to give them money, just because!

About midway through his rookie year, Glen called me and said, "Dad, money hasn't changed me, but some of our relatives are acting crazy over money! They come to me with their sob stories about all their financial problems, then I have to gauge my heart to see if they're truthful. The sad part, if I help them, the following week they're asking for more money! Where is their SELF DIGNITY?"

This was truly a lesson learned, and one that Glen had to face for himself. Glen ended our conversation by saying, "Dad, I still love them, but in order to protect myself, that love will truly be a distant one!"

I have two verses that I want to share with you. One verse shows Gods intensions and the other justifies how God has positioned us to be happy and successful.

John 10:10 tells us this: "The thief comes only to steal and kill and destroy. I came that they may have life and have it abundantly." What God is telling us in this verse is that if we don't know Him. We will truly be deceived!

Ephesians 1:3 tells us this: "Blessed be the God and Father of our Lord Jesus Christ, who has blesses us in Christ with every spiritual blessing in the heavenly realm." WOW. In this verse God is reassuring us that He has given us everything that we need to be successful!

The focal point here is that if our hearts aren't righteous, although our blessing is within arm's reach, we will never grasp it.

In other words, God creates a puzzle of abundant life and gives us all the pieces to assemble our puzzle. The faithful servants that trust God will pay attention. They will listen to Him, and ask questions, and contently wait for His answer. And inevitably they will correctly assemble their puzzle and receive the fruits that God has prepared for them.

However, the worldly participants will take their pieces of the puzzle and in a prideful manner try to force them in place therefore creating a false, twisted appearance that benefits no one.

The sad part about this barbaric behavior is that they will hand this curse down through their seed and generations to come!

Much of America's economic success is driven by greed and the desire for power and money. Our nation is obsessed with these things, and the more we get, the more we want!

Biblically speaking, boundaries are related to self-control. The Bible commands us to control ourselves, whereas our human nature desires to control others (Tit. 2:12). If left unchecked, our natural desires run roughshod over others.

Personal boundaries help to limit our selfish inclination to control or manipulate others. A person with clear, healthy boundaries communicates to others what is and is not permissible, saying in effect, "This is my jurisdiction, and you have no right to interfere!"

This is what Gods says in Matthew 6:24: "No one can serve two masters, for either he will hate the one and love the other, or he will be devoted to the one and despise the other." You cannot serve God and money!

Glen would start the 2009 NFL preseason blazing hot by being the leading rusher averaging 6.5 yards per carry.

His jaw-dropping performance would once again put him back on *Sports Illustrated* radar. Although they were preseason games, Glen was being noticed around the league. *Sports Illustrated* declared him the second-best rookie in anybody's training camp.

Many viewed Glen as the first real backup the 49ers ever had for Frank Gore! Offensive coordinator Jimmy Raye singled Glen out in remarks to protecting the quarterback with his superior pass-blocking skills.

The 49ers won three out of their four preseason games! Glen was the nucleus of the offense and led the way with his veteran-like running style. Relying on his battlefield tactics, he ran for 129 yards against Oakland and 67 against Denver.

The 49ers were definitely looking to improve from their 7–9 record from the 2008 season. Their main area of focus was enhancing their power-run game to set up the pass, and Glen was their man.

Mike Singletary was the head coach for the 49ers, and this would be his first full year after being name the interim head coach in 2008.

My first NFL experience would be August 29 at Jerry's World, 49ers vs. Cowboys, in Arlington, Texas. How can you not applaud Mr. Jerry Jones in reference to his unique stadium?

The AT&T Stadium is a city-owned, 105,000-seat capacity stadium with an in-house big screen TV and retractable roof, looking like something sprung from the imagination of the world's greatest architects. This astonishing scene is credited solely to Mr. Jones, the owner of the Dallas Cowboys.

Glen had racked up 129 yards in a previous game, that win for the 49ers really gave them a new identity. The fans really enjoyed watching the rookie from Alabama carry his portion of the load.

Seeing Glen in his new 49ers uniform was so surreal and once again he would deliver a dominating performance to help defeat the Cowboys in a 20–13 victory.

I have to admit that's the first time I've watched the entire game from the jumbotron. I started out by watching the game on the field, but the 160-foot-wide and 72-foot-tall screen is so massive that you're drawn to it. It stretches from 20 yard line to 20 yard line. One of the kickers punted the football, and it hit the corner of the screen, the officials declared a play-on because there were no rules in the playbook for that situation!

Watching the screen gives you a feeling that you're at the IMAX Theater watching the game on the big screen!

Glen would score his first career touchdown in the first quarter against the Atlanta Falcons October 11. It was also his first career start due to Frank Gore being out with an ankle injury.

The next game that I would attend would was October 25, the Houston Texans would host the 49ers at the amazing Reliant Stadium.

The 49ers put up a good fight but would suffer a loss in a close match with the Texans. The final score was 24–21.

The highlight of the game for me was that I got a chance to see Glen after the game. He was in good spirits. I always enjoy talking to him because he always has a good word of inspiration for me. I also got a chance to mingle with his teammates to get autographs, which was real cool!

I didn't know it, but even at this point in Glen's career, God was talking to him, telling him that playing football "is not what I want you to do at that point in your life!"

Although we forget sometimes, our first purpose in life is to serve Christ! Remember Jesus was GOD in the flesh and he loved us so much that he became a man and dwelled among us!

Underline this next statement: to show His true motive among all creation, He came as a helpless LAMB! Not a lion, or five-star general, or a gladiator, not even a rich CEO of a firm.

He humbled Himself, He humbled Himself, and He humbled Himself and came as a servant!

WHY? It's because of our failures and His unconditional AGAPE love for us! God had already destroyed the world once in the days of Noah. Then the children of Israel came, later called Jews, and were given the Law of Moses. Moses attempted to show the Jews right from wrong through Gods instructions. As time passed, however, they too had defiled their way.

There's an old saying that says, "If you want something done right, you have to do it yourself!"

Jesus came and used LOVE as a weapon. In Jesus Christ we have a manly example of righteousness and a role model!

We are surely responsible for the next generation. The twisted traditional lies that we have unraveled, do we continue to hand them down to our children or will we squash them under our feet and tell the truth to them?

In today's world we have been groom to be important, and we've lost the art of serving!

CHAPTER 12

God Talks to Glen

Glen finished his 2009 rookie season with 344 total yards and 1 touchdown as the second-string running back! His football IQ was telling him, "Okay, I've got my first year in the NFL under my belt now. It's a start. During the off-season I need to heal and prepare my body to finish strong!"

Playing in the backfield, Glen knew he needed to develop more lower-body power to penetrate the defensive line and game-breaking speed to reach the end zone quicker.

He shared with me that sometimes his flexibility training alone would last over two hours!

He came home prior to starting his 2010 minicamp to implement his own training program. He looked really good. We got a chance to have dinner with him and meet his trainer/nutritionist.

Playing in the pros was a new dimension, and he had truly been battle tested. I could see the professional growth in his face as he spoke with confidence and passion. His jump from high school to college was big time in terms of complexities of the game. But the transition from college to the NFL trumps all sports.

For the longest time I really felt that boxers were the ultimate warriors. After watching both of my sons play in the SEC and one in the NFL, my thought process has definitely changed. Now I salute football players.

In college Glen was competing against athletes fresh out of high school who were developing as young adults. Most were the best players on their respective teams labeled four- or five-star athletes. In the NFL, those young adults have completely developed and you're literally competing against the best two thousand or so football players in the entire world.

In this group you will face the biggest, strongest, toughest men you will ever see in your life.

The reason the NFL stands above all other sports in popularity is because players have a composition of elegance combined with brute strength, which enables them to perform at an elite supernatural level.

When I worked for the Emerald Coast YMCA, I hosted a NFL punt, pass, kick competition for youth ages six to fifteen, coed. Each year around late November, we would reward the finalist by taking them to Jacksonville, Florida, to participate in the Jaguar's halftime show.

It was such a blast and one of the highlights of my career. We'd conduct the competition early that Sunday morning, give out the awards, and then take our seats to get ready for kickoff.

At the eight-minute mark of the second quarter, we'd gather the kids and take them down to the field to prepare for our halftime show.

Being that close to the players and watching them battle really caught me off guard in a good way. The players were much bigger, faster, and stronger. It was just a tenacious scene. The field looked like it had been plowed due to bodies running, flying through the air, and massive three-hundred-pound-plus gargantuan lineman defending their turf.

A lineman's body mass combined with his speed, on an average, can produce up to 1,600 pounds of tackle force. They were hitting so hard, I could literally feel the ground move underneath my feet! Amazingly, with proper conditioning and high-tech equipment, these "gladiators" are well protected as they perform their daily jobs.

We shouldn't be surprised or intimidated by the elite stats produced by football players. Jesus has already set the tone for us. He was the superhero with six-pack abs two thousand years ago. He was a man of great stamina who chose to walk everywhere, regularly traveling over hills and mountains. He was not a bodybuilder growing his muscles with weights for show in front of mirrors; Jesus physical fitness was used in the service of others.

Finally, it was time for Glen to journey back to San Francisco for their fall training camp. We had a good dinner and talked about some future projects for the family, then wished him well on his journey.

Glen had a very productive minicamp and showed traits of greatness. He would surely be in a dogfight trying to defend his backup running back title.

He was definitely heading into a promising second year season, and everything was going so well, or so I thought.

I didn't know it at the time, but a stunning turn of events would soon take place that would shatter my world! I was at work at the Fort Walton Beach, Florida, YMCA on a typical Friday evening, just waiting to get off. I was planning on going to the beach to check out the pier and the breathtaking, enticing scenery.

Before I could walk out of my office, the phone rang. I answered the phone. It was one of my lawyer buddies. In a very exhilarated voice, he said, "Glen, I'm watching CNN live, and your son just announced his retirement from the 49ers!" There was silence on my part. I was speechless, discombobulated. I felt like I had just taken a blow to the gut. Finally, I murmured some words. "What? What?

WHAT do you mean?" He replied, "Yeah, man, I'm just as shocked as you are!" At this point I was very concerned about Glen and confused.

I told my friend that as soon as I got off the phone with him that I'd call Glen and get on top of this situation, giving him the impression that I was going to fix everything. I hung up my office phone and walked outside to call Glen on my cell.

I was frantic at this point, worried, and didn't have a clue why Glen would do something like this without talking to me first!

I immediately called Glen, and he was still in the press conference. We briefly talked but in seemed like an eternity. I just wanted to make sure he was okay, and I asked him, "Son, are you all right?"

He responded, "Yes, Dad, I'm good."

Of course, I asked him why did he retire.

He said, "Dad, I can't talk long, but I was in the practice field locker room last night and GOD came to me and started talking to my heart!"

Glen told me that GOD instructed him to retire from the NFL and go out into the world and spread His word! Glen told me that he tried to rationalize with God by saying, "All my life I have wanted to be a professional football player, and You want me to give this life up. I CAN'T DO THAT, GOD!"

After trying to negotiate with God, Glen told me that He came at him straight up by saying, "You say that you love me, then give up football, all of it, the money and the fame. I AM GOD!

Finally Glen submitted to God and surrendered his heart to him by saying, "Okay, GOD, here I am. I'm yours!"

As Glen's story was unfolding, all of a sudden my worries went away and were replaced with a warm, peaceful, confident, satisfying feeling. It was as though I had been clothed with a fresh ocean breeze!

Unexpectedly, I started crying. They weren't just a couple of tear drops. Out of nowhere, I burst into a helpless cry and was shedding a whole river of tears. I never cry. I was raised prideful. I remember growing up, the only time I faked a cry was when I had to fight my oldest brother. My mom would come home from work, then I'd fake a cry so she would handle him!

So I was at work weeping like a child in front of all my coworkers, talking to my son, it was embarrassing. I tried to stop crying, but the tears kept coming and the snot kept flowing from my nose!

To add to the unusual chain of events, a voice came to me and said, "Support your son!"

Miraculously, I realized I was in the presence of the Holy Spirit and I trembled with fear! I just didn't expect GOD to dial in, of all people! You know how we are. We only want GOD in our lives when it's convenient for us. We use Him, then we put Him back in the cupboard.

The omnipotent, omnipresent GOD had His hand on me. I felt as though I was in the garden just walking and talking with God! Someone as high as He would reach down to somebody as low as me and share a message. My emotions were all over the place. I felt blessed, and then I trembled because I knew God was totally aware of my dark side as well!

Although I felt unworthy in His presence, Jesus saw the best in me and gave me a dose of righteousness so potent that it brought me to my knees!

Finally, I summed up enough courage to asked God what was my role in Glen's retirement? He responded, "Tell your son's story!"

I knew Glen couldn't talk long. Before I got off the phone, I told him that he did the right thing by following God's instructions. I also asked him to pray for me, and he responded by saying, "I got you, Dad!"

At this point my coworkers were very concerned and worried about my emotional breakdown. I assured them that I was okay and told them that Glen had retired from the NFL but he was okay.

The moment of disbelief in their faces quickly followed with a bombardment of questions. I felt dog tired and drained physically and mentally. To avoid any further questions, I informed them that I'd brief them Monday morning.

Of course, they were huge fans of Glen and I felt they were entitled to hear what had taken place.

To say the least those plans for going to the beach would not take place. When I got home I prayed and just tried to process and wrap my head around what had just taken place. Eventually, I just went to sleep.

I woke up the next morning in a state of denial, hoping that it all was just a bad dream!

The reality is that on Friday, August 13, 2010, Glen would shock the NLF nation by announcing his retirement from the San Francisco 49ers after playing only one season!

As Christian parents, we raise our children to serve God, be independent, have successful careers, and hopefully pray about important decisions and act on them. At some point in our parenthood status, we have to respect the decisions of our GROWN children!

I have to admit when I initially called Glen I was concerned about his welfare. However, a part of me wanted to say, "What in the hell is wrong with you?" Thankfully, before I could utter those words, God converted my selfish heart to a humble one! After I sat and rehashed my conversation with Glen, I'm extremely thankful that he did not call me and ask for my opinion because I'm not God!

Glen called me later that day, and we had a lengthy discussion about his retirement. He shared with me that he had been "wrestling" with the decision for some time. He had come to the conclusion that God had another plan for him. He told me the evening prior to his retirement that he was fully dressed getting ready to hit the practice field, then God came to him. So he waited until the locker room emptied and was sitting there talking to God and staring at the tape on his football cleats.

Glen told God, "Okay, God, if I cut this tape from my cleats, I'm walking away from football!" So Glen cut the tape and took off his practice uniform and went home. He told me when he cut the tape from his cleats that it felt as if a huge weight had been lifted from his back and he was at peace!

Later on that night, around 11:00 p.m., Glen heard a knock at his door. It was the training staff, and they were concerned because Glen hadn't notified anyone about his departure. Glen informed his trainers why he left abruptly, and they said, "Okay, we have to call Coach Singletary immediately!"

They called Coach Singletary, and he said, "All right, we'll have a meeting first thing in the morning!" Surprisingly, Coach Singletary told Glen that he appreciated his honesty and not just coming out and going through the motions. "All this means is that you're not supposed to be here, and that someone else is supposed to be in your place!"

Coach Nick Saban said he was really surprised and that Glen was such a warrior-type competitor when he was there.

Before I got off the phone with Glen, he said, "Dad, a lot of people aren't going to understand and realize because they don't have wisdom to understand. Their eyes aren't open like mine are open! True happiness is glorifying God and Christ."

I said good-bye to Glen, and I told him that I loved him. I understood his calling and just wanted to support him in any way that I could.

It was a gorgeous Saturday in Florida, but I wasn't ready to go out and face the community yet, my phone was already ringing every five minutes!

Several channels were still covering Glen's story, and they were pretty grim, I thought. The media can really be a display of savagery at times. One reporter asked Glen, "Why can't you be like Tim Tebow—play football, worship God, and get paid at the same time?" Glen responded, "First, I'm not Tim Tebow. I walked away from football because I submitted to God's will. In order to have a quality life one must have peace in their heart. My peace is serving Christ! There's more to life than the pursuit of money!"

Glen's retirement really awakened me from a daze in relation to my faith. While Glen was serving this world everything was great, normal protocol! However, when he surrendered his heart to Christ and does something out of the norm, it's a huge problem!

God put Glen on a public platform so He could demonstrate His power in him. When Glen announced his retirement, the devil fell off his thrown and ran and hid like the coward he is!

As Christians, we are constantly in the midst of haters, naysayers, racist, and people that don't even like their own dog.

When God has us no one can touch us, broken life and all. In this world, anytime we stand up for Christ, we will surely face persecution and that's okay!

Glen's retirement gave birth to an enormous blessing, and it was prime time for us to get on our knees and glorify God.

In 1 Peter 2:9 God tells us that "we are a chosen people, a royal priesthood, a Holy nation, a people belonging to God, that you may declare the praises of him that brought you out of the darkness into His wonderful light."

We are called for the purpose of praising God and worshipping God. That is one of the job descriptions of a Christian.

The reality is that we as Christians label God as our good buddy or friend. We go back and forth, in and out, and up and down in our relationship with Him! It's called Christian arrogance, yet He still loves us!

After watching Glen's interview, I decided to turn the TV off and just meditate and bask in God's glory, just praising Him. So I was sitting there, and I thought, *My son is a modern-day saint! I've never met anyone in my entire life that pursues God's love the way he does!*

God gave us the Book of Job as a tool to measure our faith. In the Book of Genesis, God gave us Abraham, the father of all nations, and Joseph, the prince of Egypt. All these prophets trusted, feared, loved, and believed in God! However, when they shared their faith with their family members, they became very jealous, envious, and hostile!

In John 7:5 Jesus's own brothers didn't believe in Him, even after living with Him for thirty years!

Glen knew he had to face the "mob" after making his decision—the angry fans, the thirsty media, and the lost relatives. Even in the midst of his persecution, he did not flinch because he knew God had his back! WOW, that's so powerful!

The weekend was over, and it was time for me to head to work. I got up and got prayed up and went to work Monday around 9:00 a.m.

I knew it was going to be a tasking day just as I had anticipated. I was getting some interesting looks and greetings as I approached my office.

My coworkers held out as long as they could. It was just a matter of time before they demanded to hear why Glen really retired. It felt like my phone rang from 9:00 a.m. to 5:00 p.m. I had a parade in and out of my office, even the daily newspaper called for an interview.

I didn't mind answering their questions. In this crazy world that we live in today, I was honored that Glen was man enough to stand for Jesus! The sad part was that most of the feedback was in reference to money or when is he coming back to the league. One would think that the main topic here is God. I'm just saying!

To testify and show the power of God, I told Glen's story to my seven-year-old niece one day.

Remarkably her response caught me totally off guard. She asked me, "How does one know if God is talking to them?"

I was really searching for an answer that she would understand. Within seconds God put the perfect answer on my heart to give to her. I responded, "When you see a butterfly, how does it make you feel?"

She said, "Very happy."

I went on to tell her, "Sometimes things happen in our lives that make us sad. Because God doesn't want us to be sad, He loves us so much that, if we just call His name, he will come into our hearts and make us feel happy and safe."

She said, "Thank you, Uncle Glen. I understand now."

God is always talking to us. The question that we need to ask ourselves is, Are we tuned in to the right channel to receive His message?

If you've watched the sun come up or set in its beautiful horizon or felt the calm of the wind, God is communicating with you.

In John 10:27 God says, "But because you are not my sheep, you refuse to believe. My sheep listen to my voice; I know them and they follow me. And I give them eternal life and they will never perish. No one can snatch them out of my hand."

Let us all learn from this exuberant message and how to respond to God's blessings, especially the blessing of salvation.

Do you really think God would dwell in us and not communicate with us? God speaks to us all the time, and he's speaking to us now!

I didn't see this coming, but another blessing that sprung out of Glen's retirement was the way I was viewed in the public eye! Before, my public title was Glen's and Matt's dad! After Glen's retirement, my unofficial title quickly changed to the holy father!

It was a great honor, but the truth of the matter is that, even today I sometimes fall physically and spiritually. But you can guarantee if I fall, I get right back up, because I don't have to wait for the world to pat me on the back or tell me that I'm special. I know for fact that my Father in heaven loves me unconditionally.

My title at the Fort Walton YMCA was associate branch/sports director. I really grew up a lot in relation to human values during my time with the Y! That experience positioned me to help raise and be a role model for so many youth in our community!

One day a lady rushed in my office, and I could clearly see that she was very upset. Erratically she said, "Mr. Coffee, you've done such a great job with Glen! I'm a single mother, and I'm having so much trouble with my fourteen-year-old son! He's so disrespectable. He even yells at me and is totally out of control!" Then she began to weep bitterly, catching me totally off guard, but I didn't let her know that. After I got her to calm down, she pleaded with me to allow her son to volunteer at the Y so I could mentor him.

I definitely felt her pain and truly wanted to help. Being a not-for-profit organization, we wouldn't be effective without volunteers.

I agreed to her request and developed a schedule for her son. His name was Seth. After meeting him, I discovered that he really wasn't a bad kid at all. He just needed some godly guidance, just like we all do. After talking to Seth, I discovered that his grades were down and he really didn't have any goals.

I wanted to be genuine with him by sharing my story about the emptiness and feeling short changed by not having a father around. And how the wisdom from the Bible really gave me fulfillment and put me on the right path.

I told Seth that I hoped our relationship would be long-term, and that I wanted to support his growth and development in all categories of his life.

After Seth completed his volunteer training course, he started out by helping with my youth sports program.

Our mission statement at the Y was to put Christian principles into practice through programs that build healthy spirit, mind, and body for all.

All our sports were developmental. Meaning, winning or losing was not our focus! We ensured that all participants would have equal playing time regardless of talent level.

The younger kids really liked Seth, and he loved working with them. We would take a knee and pray before all games. Seth would lead us in prayer sometimes. It was a blessing seeing him grow into his purpose.

One day Seth came in and said, "Mr. Coffee, my grades are really good in school now. I may even go out for the varsity football team!" I was so happy for Seth. As I look back, I realize my adolescence was a reflection of his. I'm just so happy that I was able to give back!

The word *mentor* is defined as a wise and trusted counselor or teacher.

Jesus mentored His disciples. Christian mentoring is a process dependent upon submission to Christ. Neither the mentor nor the candidate controls the relationship. The mentor serves as a model and a trusted listener. The mentor relies on the Holy Spirit to provide insight to change lives.

Later on Seth came by to thank me for the bond that we had given birth to. His mother also called with praises.

Sometimes when we rewind the wheel of life, there are parts that we wish we could take back. This episode with Seth was so humbling for me, and I'm so thankful I was fortunate enough to give back this time, instead of another regret! Glory be to God!

CHAPTER 13

The 700 Club

The 700 Club is the flagship program of the Christian Broadcasting Network, airing throughout the United States and available worldwide on CBN.com.

Airing each weekday, the news magazine program features live guests, daily news, contemporary music, testimonies, and Christian lifestyle issues.

The network has been in production since 1966 and has aired for over thirty-eight years on the same network. It is hosted by Pat Robertson, Gordon Robertson, Terry Meeuwsen, and Wendy Griffith.

At this point Glen's unique story has stretched around the globe. Recognizing the significance of his retirement, *The 700 Club* invited him on their show November 25, 2010, to meet him and hear his courageous testimony.

Before we dive into Glen's interview, I want to vigorously point out some topics of vital importance so we all can wrap our heads around what really took place in reference to his retirement.

Okay, first, God is omnipotent. He knows all. He's omnipresent. He's everywhere all the time. He's the Alpha and Omega, the beginning and end of all things.

This means that our time and God's time are totally different. God doesn't wear a watch or have clocks hanging on His wall. He's just sitting back, chilling, waiting, for us to get in the game.

When we think we have everything figured out, He'll ruffle some feathers, pick a fight, and throw us right in the middle of it. The reason is that He wants to change the direction of our path and get our attention for His glory.

God will purposely snatch us and confuse us so that we will seek Him for understanding. We look in all the wrong places when our hearts are troubled. Being at the hottest concert tour, or listening to a presidential speech, or even at a football game are all thrilling; however, the only way to mend a broken heart is when we come to Jesus!

When I went to Jesus with my broken heart in relation to Glen's retirement, this is what God shared with me: God commanded Glen to give up his most valuable possession, football, to test his faith. Just as he commanded Abraham to sacrifice his son Isaac as a burnt offering to test his faith. Why? Because God had a higher calling for them and wanted to bless them.

Jeremiah 29:11 states, "I know what I'm doing. I have it all planned out—plans to take care of you, not abandon you, plans to give the future you hoped for."

Glen's reporter was Mr. Shawn Brown from CBN Sports. He started the interview with a well-planned strategic approach. He started out by commending Glen for his undeniable potential to become one of the league's top running backs. But on the brink of the 2010 season, Glen shocked the pro football world by walking away from the sport at twenty-three years old.

Of course, the question on everyone's mind was why. Why walk away from the lucrative contracts and a lifetime dream?

Here was Glen's comments:

Going into my sophomore season, I hurt my knee. I was going to miss the whole year, and until that point, I entered college thinking I was going to be an All-American, All-SEC (Southeastern Conference) and all that. It wasn't happening for me, so I was at a point in my life where I was like, "What now?" You know, my whole life everything I did was football. Eat football, sleep football, and wake in the morning thinking about football. It wasn't happening like I had planned.

I didn't take school seriously in high school or college because football was my only ticket.

During my recovery, I got a new roommate. I started to realize that this guy had confidence. It wasn't worldly. It was coming from something else. So I just set down one day, and I was like, "What is it?" And he told me why he lived. He told me that he was on this earth to glorify God and that's it, you know.

"Finally, man," I said. "Christ, I need You in my life. I need You! I tried the other route. I tried football. So I asked Him into my life, and it was just a 180. Everything I did was for Him and for His Glory."

As soon as I became a Christian, all of my priorities in life changed.

Football was no longer first. Christ was first, you know, and a couple of other things... family, friends. And football fell down the ladder. So one day I told Him, "Christ, look you've got me playing football. I don't necessarily love football anymore. It was no longer my dream."

If I'm out here playing, I'm going to do the best I can to glorify You. So I need Your help.

Every yard I gained was for His glory. When I was on the field, I honestly felt that if you tackled me you were trying to stop me from my ministry. Because I knew that the more media attention I got, the more I could deflect towards Him. And so I had that season and it was a great feeling. But even in having that season I still knew in my heart that football wasn't it.

I was still struggling with leaving my dream of playing professional football behind. So I left school early and entered the 2009 NFL Draft.

I was doing what the world expected me to do. What my family and friends expected me to do. All I had known was football. So to say I was thinking about walking away was scary!

I tried to rationalize it. I said, "Okay, God. I did it in college. Let's do it again. But my heart wasn't in it. I was trying to talk myself up. I was trying to talk myself into it. It was hard, real hard! Because when you don't listen to God's will and you do what the world expects you to do, you never reach what you're trying to reach. You're always struggling. You're in the water, and you're always trying to stay afloat.

I battled my rookie season out on the grid-iron. But it was nothing compared to the battle going on inside. To ease my mind, I threw myself into the lavish lifestyle of a pro athlete.

So I got the money, and I started to splurge just a little bit to try to catch a feeling, to find some happiness. I knew money didn't buy happiness, but I was going to try to find something. There had to be a reason why everybody's chasing money. I could never find it. I'd buy this or get that or have this, and it didn't mean anything.

When I reported to our 2010 training camp, I realized that I had to face a tough decision. I had told Coach Singletary and my teammates that I was going to ride or die with them for at least four years. Then maybe think about my career after that. But it was burning inside me.

He's telling you to do something. You don't listen, so now I'm in this position, so now I've got to make a decision.

I continued through training camp hoping what I felt would go away. But it didn't. One day before practice, I came to a crossroad.

Getting up in the morning was just hard. It wasn't because I was tired. I was tired spiritually. When you fight God and you're off the kingdom, you're going to lose that battle eventually. It's going to wear down on your spirit. It's going to wear down on you mentally, physically, all that. And it got to the point to where I just couldn't take it.

I went into the locker room. It's like five minutes before practice. I was sitting there, and I looked down at my cleats, and I'm thinking. If I cut this tape from my cleats, I won't have time to retape them. I'm really going to walk away. I get the tape cutters, and I cut the tape off my cleats. It was like a gorilla jumping off my back.

Now I'm fighting for souls. I'm not fighting for a victory. I'm not fighting for a game. I'm fighting for souls right now. Christ is everlasting. He'll never let you down. He's always got your back. So follow His will, and you'll be fine!

CHAPTER 14

Inspirational Speaker

Let's pause for a minute and sing and dance for God right now. Because you know He's right there in the room and there in your heart just loving you!

Our omnipotent God is so clever. Now He has put Glen on a worldwide platform and sent him out to preach His living word.

In the twisted world that we live in today, if Glen wasn't famous, do you really think he would have an audience?

Even if we hated God and He wanted us to join His ranks, we would fall to our knees and worship Him.

In his quest to serve God, Glen traveled the nation, speaking at business conferences, churches, youth groups, Fellow Christian Athletes (FCA), etc. I attended several of his speaking engagements.

He's a very dynamic speaker. His topics are crystal clear, and he speaks with a very eloquent tone. As I reminisce, one of his best works was when he spoke to two-thousand-plus Christian youth at the Emerald Coast Worship Center in our hometown in Fort Walton Beach, Florida.

As Glen addressed the youth, his main topics were drugs, sex, alcohol, and bullying. While addressing the issue of abstinence, I really appreciated the way he came down to their level.

He started out by telling them during his junior year at Fort Walton High School, he and the football team where in the locker room one day. A younger sophomore player approached him in a boastful manner and said, "Hey, Glen, I just had sex last night and you're a junior and you still haven't got laid yet!" Glen went on to say that, that one comment hurt him to the core and he had to take that blow on the chin all by himself. Glen went on to say, "I wasn't grounded in Christ. The only thing I had to say was, "Hey, bro, I'm not about that. I serve a mighty God, and I'm about His business."

Glen told his audience that after that day his number one goal in life was to get laid! When we don't have Christ in our lives, the devil has free reign over us, free reign! Clearly, thankfully, at a young age Glen respectfully understood that flaunting and parading girls around was not acceptable. However, peer pressure and temptation haunts us all.

Another testimony that Glen shared and one that really made me stand up in my seat was when he, Matt, and I would have home Bible studies. When they were younger, I would conduct a family Bible study with them, and they really enjoyed hearing about Jesus. However, when I returned from my second tour in Saudi Arabia, we did resume our Bible studies but Glen's heart wasn't in it. It was a direct reflection of how much of the world he had become!

At that this point in Glen's life, Jesus had become just a TV character. Glen also revealed to the crowd that he really wanted to tell me that he just wasn't interested in hearing about Jesus! I'm glad he kept that thought to himself! As he was telling this particular story, I wanted to slide down in my seat and hide because I didn't even know that he felt that way about Jesus. Glen did shed some light by sharing this verse with the crowd: "It is the Lord who goes before you. He will be with you; He will never leave you or forsake you. Do not fear or be dismayed" (Deut. 31:8).

I'm so, so thankful for God's everlasting love. The fact of the matter is that we are ordinary people placed in extraordinarily circumstances sometimes. Glen's story reveals that even when he was wandering in the world, God's love is constant and merciful, regardless of our actions. The audience applauded Glen for his sincere testimonies!

I was truly convicted upon hearing his testimonies. They just made me want to be a better person in every category of life.

After Glen's speaking engagement, he was blessed even further. All the youth lined up to greet him, and they were just lamenting, repenting, and thanking him. They also assured him that they would adopt a better life that would glorify God!

A while later I received an unusual phone call from Glen. I answered the phone, and he said, "Dad, I'm in jail!"

I responded jokingly like, "Yeah, right."

He said, "No, I'm serious!"

Of course, I cautiously asked, "Why are you in jail?"

He replied, "I just got back in town from a speaking engagement, and I was speeding. When the policeman stopped me, they discovered that my registration and insurance had expired, and they had to tow my vehicle."

So I asked him, "Why were you driving with suspended documents?"

He said, "Dad, I know I made a mistake. I was going to get them renewed as soon as I got back in town."

At this point I asked him if he needed anything, and he responded, "No, Dad, I've got to spend the night in jail. I'll be out in the morning."

I was upset at Glen, but he was a grown man, also an awesome son. I figured one night in jail wouldn't hurt anything.

Glen told me later that his cellmate recognized him and asked him, "Hey, bro, are you Glen Coffee?" Glen said he tried to ignore him, but before he could answer, his cellmate started yelling at the top of his voice, "Hey, y'all. Hey, y'all, I'm in the cell with Glen Coffee!" "Yeah, yeah, the one that played football for Alabama and the 49ers!"

I went to bed that night telling myself that this will surely be a lesson that Glen will learn from.

The next morning I was awaken with a barrage of phone calls with friends asking me had I seen the newspaper and why was Glen being charged with carrying and illegal weapon.

So I went and got a paper and the headline read: "Glen Coffee Ex-NFL Star Busted with Cocked hand gun!"

At this point I was fulminating and ready to explode with anger. The whole state of Florida knew Glen and knew that he stood for Christ! I was asking myself why this propaganda was being printed about my son. But deep down inside I knew the answer! Once again in this world we will serve Jesus or Satan.

In Matthew 25:31 Jesus tells us that He's coming to separate the sheep from the goats. In John 1:29 John the Baptist tells the world, "Behold, the Lamb of God," referring to Jesus. So we need to be sheep, right? Because we have titles, that doesn't necessarily qualify us as legit leaders!

There's no greater power than God! It doesn't matter what man says, God will have the last say!

I'm sure at that point the devil was jumping for joy, thinking he had taken our joy away!

So I called Glen and said, "Man, have you seen the paper?"

He replied, "Yeah, Dad."

And, of course, I asked him about the false allegations that were printed in the newspaper!

He calmly said, "Calm down, Dad. I've already prayed about it, and God has our back."

WOW, you got to love this kid!

Glen told me that the officer informed him that they were going to tow his truck. Prior to towing it, without even asking, they searched his truck and discovered his handgun in the center console. At this point the officer drew his weapon and arrested Glen!

A while back Glen was at a gas station in Alabama and was approached by a gunman attempting to rob him! Due to his immense traveling as a motivational speaker, he purchased a gun to protect himself.

To set the record straight, the policeman found Glen's 380 SIG SAUER semiautomatic pistol in the center console of his 2008 Cadillac Escalade. The chamber was empty and the cocked hammer is a safety feature, the only way to fire the weapon is to release the hammer, load the chamber, then the weapon is ready to fire.

Thankfully, the judge dismissed the mute case based on an inaccurate report!

The fact that Glen was adored by many and had earned undeniable popularity on the football field and never been in any trouble, one would think that the media would favor him? For example, the newspaper could have easily stated: "Glen Coffee the Ex-NFL Star has been arrested and charged with a crime that does not fit his character. Let's pray for a godly outcome on his behalf."

I'm just saying!

I have to admit that I initially responded with a worldly rage when I first saw the newspaper. And I apologize for that. After the dust had settled, Glen and I had time to reboot, meditate, and pray about what had taken place. Then God blessed me by sending me a glorious revelation!

There was someone at the jail that God wanted Glen to minister to. And, oh yes, because Glen was their special guest, you know they gave him the royal treatment. You know, bend down, touch the toes, here come the old BODY CAVITY CHECK!

Glen told me that he felt as low as dog and violated. But as soon as the show was over, Glen waited for his queue, politely raised his hand, and said, "Hey, y'all, I know a man name Jesus and He is the truth! He's your peace, joy, happiness. And He will wipe all your tears away."

Glen, being a soldier for Christ, was totally focused on His Father's business. He didn't have time to be mad at anyone! Glen told me that he ministered to his cellmate and anyone that came in contact with him!

As Christians we're programmed to serving God under our terms, in our comfort zone, in the cool A/C on a Sunday morning, or at the beach, or while shopping. God will profoundly point you in a direction and send you to places you don't want to go.

As long as you feel that you're richer, better and more important than everyone else, you aren't the one God is looking for!

The world will use, abuse, steal from you, and try to take your soul. But God tells us, "Fear not my faithful servants, for the harvest is indeed plentiful, but the laborers are few. And because of your faithful, continued service, I'm going to bless you like you've never been blessed before."

The officers that God commissions are well screened and battle-tested. They are honorable, humble, resilient, and fearless. If you're not ready, God will not ask you to conquer a fully armed giant with a slingshot.

The next event where I watched Glen speak was at the Choctawhatchee High School football stadium. The main audience consisted of high school students and Fellow Christian Athlete (FCA) members. It was a concert-type setting with a huge stage and electrifying gospel band.

After an awesome praise and worship service, Glen started his message out by saying: "When you are working for the Kingdom, there are a lot of things that you have to sacrifice. Even when my body is torn battered and bruised, I still want to hear my number called in the huddle because it gives me one more chance to run for—and toward—my Heavenly Father. If you are willing to accept Jesus Christ into your heart and into your life and would like to become a fellow player with me on God's Kingdom-building team, you can pray a simple prayer like, 'Jesus I know that I am a sinner. And because sin separates me from you, I deserve death. I believe that You are Lord and that You came to this earth to die in my place and to conquer death, so that I may receive eternal life. Please come into my heart and change my life so that I may become a new creation in Christ Jesus. I thank you for giving me this new life. Amen!'"

Glen delivered his message, which was a topic about our salvation. He used the verses from Ephesians 2:8–9, "For by grace are ye saved through faith; and not of works, lest any man should boast." My God, that's some mighty good word right there!

We truly need to highlight and meditate on this part.

Let's focus on grace for a moment. In the New Testament grace means God's love in action toward men who merited the opposite of love.

Grace means God moving heaven and earth to save sinners who couldn't lift a finger to save themselves.

Grace means God sending His only son to descend into hell on the cross so that we guilty ones might be reconciled to God and received into heaven.

The promise to the believer is sealed with the Holy Spirit as a guarantee that one day Jesus the Christ will return to claim His bride! (Eph. 1:12–14, 4:30).

God's intimate, profound, promiscuous grace is unrestrained! Meaning that He is giving it away so freely that it's unmerited and we can get it anywhere, anytime!

We are saved by God's merciful grace and not of our own efforts! Can you imagine if there was a million-dollar bounty that we had to pay to get into heaven? Or how do you even put a cash value on eternal life?

In order for us to really receive the fruits that God has prepared for us, we need to look in the mirror and claim our true identity. If it needs to be fixed, fix it. If it isn't broken, leave it alone.

In reference to our relationship with God, we all basically fall into three different classes.

First, we have the natural man. In 1 Corinthians 2:14 the apostle Paul tells us that the natural man receives "not the things of the spirit of God: for they are foolishness unto him." Meaning that if God hugs, talks, or even taps him on the shoulder, he wouldn't receive any of those things because he's totally disconnected from God.

Next, we have the carnal man. This is the stage where most Christians hover. In 1 Corinthians, Apostle Paul says to the carnal Corinthian Christians: "And I brethren, could not speak to you as spiritual people, but as to carnal, as babes in Christ. I fed you with milk and not with solid food, for until now you were not able to receive it." The carnal man believes in God but still worries and is distracted and enticed by worldly temptations. If you're going to worry, don't pray. If you pray, don't worry!

Now we have the spiritual man. The spiritual man loves God first, before mommy and daddy, the children, even his money. His love for God is so unconditional that he loves God with all his heart, all his soul, all his strength, and all his mind. This type of love binds the adversary.

The spiritual man will be blessed with an abundant lifestyle and receive all the fruits of the spirit that God has prepared for him.

Glen's audience received his message with praises. It was such a blessing to see him praying, repenting, lamenting, and just demonstrating God's love.

The blessings of the struggle remove our dependence and reliance on all of our man-made safety nets. The blessing of the struggle places all focus on God and what he can do in our lives as opposed to us and what we can do for ourselves.

After that speech, Glen told me something very remarkable. He said, "Dad, I don't want to be remembered just as a great football player. I also wanted to be remembered as a man that feared God!"

If you ever get a chance to meet Glen Coffee Jr., I really pray that you see the God in him first then you can talk about the football player in him!

CHAPTER 15

Glen Joins the United States Army

Glen still travels the nation spreading seeds of salvation. He also does an outstanding job caring for his daughter, Ms. Ava Coffee, my beautiful granddaughter.

Upon Glen's retirement, of course, God called him to preach his word; but God also called him to protect His spiritual kingdom here on earth.

Let's discuss spiritual kingdom for a moment. In Habakkuk 2:14 God tells us the point of Pentecost is mission and the goal of mission is that the "earth will be filled with the knowledge of the glory of the Lord, as the waters cover the sea."

Before, Jesus physically walked with us; now He is in us. Therefore, we are his spiritual kingdom on earth. Hopefully, when we get to heaven, we'll be able to talk with the prophets! Maybe we can asked the apostle Paul or John the Baptist how was it to walk with our Lord and Savior, and in return maybe they'll ask us, "How was it to have Jesus living in our hearts?"

God loves us so much that he created us to have free will to make choices. There are some things that God allows us to do, even though he doesn't like them.

As long as there have been people, there have been misunderstandings, disagreements, fights, and wars! The Bible was written so we could see how God is involved in the lives of people in all sorts of situations, including wars!

In Matthew 24:6–8 Jesus says this: "You will hear wars and rumors of wars, but see to it that you are not alarmed. Such things must happen, but the end is still to come. Nation will rise against nation, and kingdom against kingdom. There will be famines and earthquakes in various places. All these are the beginning of birth pains." My God!

Unfortunately, in this world we are watching a growing trend of rejecting the idea that Christ is coming back literally, physically, to rule the world.

When I first joined the Air Force, my focus was serving our country and taking advantage of a secure career. I took an oath, but I'm so grateful now because it's crystal clear to me that I was serving a greater cause, which was fulfilling God's will.

Without a doubt, we must all agree that the all Armed Forces, including the police department, have a biblical obligation first! If God didn't allow us to kill our enemies, there would be no America or even freedom as we know it today. Murder and killing are two totally different animals!

We are always at war physically or spiritually.

You would think that our spiritual battles are easily fought because we know Jesus has defeated Satan! Wrong! This is how we Christians screw up! When important issues surface in our world and the topic is up for discussion, a lot of Christians give their opinions instead of quoting Scripture!

Do you really think God needs our opinion? When we give our opinion, we are simply taking sides in a debate. But when we quote Scripture, the glory goes to God. When God receives His glory, in return He shares it with us.

The gospel demands us to follow Jesus; however, when we read His word, we come to the conclusion that this task is too difficult. Therefore, we only adopt parts of the Scripture that accommodate our lavish lifestyles.

God purposely sets boundaries in the Bible because he wants us to be happy. He knows us better than we know ourselves. All Bible scripture is inspired by God and is useful to teach us what is true and make us realize what is wrong in our lives. It corrects us when we are wrong and teaches us to do what is right (2 Tim. 3:16).

Many Christians think that all they need is the New Testament. They seem to think that the Old Testament does not apply to us in this age. The relation between our Lord's teaching and that of the Old Testament is cleared up by our Lord in a striking sentence: "Don't think that I came to destroy the Law, or the prophets. I didn't come to destroy, but to fulfill" (Matt. 5:17). Jesus came to fulfill the predictions of the prophets who had long foretold that a Savior would one day appear.

God left his Living Word with us so we would know which direction to turn when problems arise. However, when we reject the truth, it simply gets us in trouble. Hosea 4:6 reads: "My people are destroyed for lack of knowledge: Because thou hast rejected knowledge, I will also reject thee!" In our country today, we have deliberately forsaken the Holy God of the Bible. We kicked God and prayer out of our public schools. By throwing God out of our public schools, we have invited the devil into our children's lives.

Being led by the Holy Spirit, Glen enlisted in the military, February 4, 2013, as an Army Ranger.

The United States Army Ranger School is an intense sixty-one-day combat leadership course oriented toward small-unit tactics. It has been called the most physically and mentally demanding leadership school the Army has to offer. It is open to soldiers, sailors, airmen, and Marines in the US Armed Forces.

Glen completed his boot camp at Fort Benning, Georgia. Fort Benning supports more than 120,000 active-duty military, reserve-component soldiers, retirees, and civilians on a daily basis.

Glen was so excited with his tremendous task at hand. When I talked to him about his new career, I could sense the adrenaline rush, as though he was preparing for a big game.

Glen would be trained in combat-arms-related functional skills. The Rangers primary mission is to engage in close combat and direct-fire battles. His training course included three different phases: crawl, walk, and run phase.

The crawl phase lasted twenty days. It's designed to assess and develop the necessary physical and mental skills to complete combat mission and the remainder of Ranger School successfully.

The walk phase takes place in the mountains and lasts twenty-one days. During this phase, students receive instructions on military mountaineering tasks as well as techniques for employing squads and platoons for continuous combat patrol operations.

The run phase continues to develop the Ranger student's combat arms functional skills. They must be capable of operating effectively under conditions of extreme mental and physical stress.

Training at the Ranger School is a prerequisite for soldiers to complete Airborne School.

To become a US Army Ranger the country's finest soldiers willingly submit themselves to what many would consider a form of torture.

They run combat missions twenty hours a day while consuming just enough calories to keep from passing out. The US Army Rangers are highly trained killing machines. They go in first. They kill. They destroy. They disappear!

The woods are a Ranger's sanctuary. Glen told me that he spent so much time in the woods that he fell in love with its natural beauty. Being among the hissing snakes, other reptiles, and all the creepy, crawling creatures became a walk in the park for him.

As part of his survival training, Glen was dropped in the middle of the forest at night alone. Being miles away from his camp, his mission was to maneuver his way back with minimal equipment.

Glen told me that he thrived during these times because of his appreciation for Mother Nature. He would often revert to his stealth mode to interact with the animals. He said often deer would walk right past him, squirrels, rabbits, and all kind of creatures.

In a mysterious way, Glen said he felt that the forest had created its own language and was trying to communicate with him. Trees are a representation of strength and constancy. For many this can bring on a sense of peace and connection when spending time around trees.

Our omnipotent God has placed Glen on yet another platform, the United States Army. After spending countless hours in the Georgia swamp with snakes and alligators, now Glen is seconds away from completing his last jump that will give him his wings!

He was in the last phase of his training with the 507th Parachute Infantry Regiment at Fort Benning, Georgia. The school is also called jump school.

Jump school certifies its students in the use of parachutes for combat situations. It is reported to be one of the toughest specialized training schools used by the Army and has bred a culture of aggressive training.

Regardless of their branch of service, all graduates receive the United States Army Parachute Badge, which is often called Jump Wings!

Glen graduated from Airborne School June 2013 and enrolled at Fort Bragg, North Carolina, to become a member of the elite US Army Special Forces.

Upon his graduation, reporters caught up with him and he gave a brief interview:

> I've always considered myself a warrior, somebody who would fight for what he believed in. It hit me like, what do you think the military does, and what do you think the military is full of? Warriors! All of a sudden, I had this respect for the military, and I just realized that there is no America without the men and women who serve this country. I figured that if I'm able, the Lord has blessed me with an able body while I'm young to get out there and get dirty.

The Bible teaches us that as Christians we should give up our lives and submit fully to the will of God!

Truly, our lives should be an illustration of Jesus walking with the cross. The men and women in the Armed Forces sacrifice their lives on a daily basis in order for us to have life. Why? Yes, we do focus on the frightful, humiliating, gruesome death that Jesus endured. The faithful servants in the military understand that, that's NOT how the story ends! Through faith, they understand that Jesus conquered the sting of death and after three days rose and walked the earth.

Our time here on earth is temporary, as in a blink of the eye, but through Jesus Christ, we have everlasting life!

Eternal life is the life of God, the Eternal One!

CHAPTER 16

After the Military

Fate, God, would bring Glen back to his origin of birth, Eglin Air Force Base, Florida, and his hometown, Fort Walton Beach, Florida. Fort Walton is only minutes from Eglin Air Force Base. After spending a couple of years in Fort Bragg, North Carolina, Glen applied for orders to transfer to Eglin.

This transfer would be a huge blessing because it would allow him to be a better provider for his young daughter, who lives in Fort Walton Beach.

Eglin Air Force Base is located in Northwest Florida, comprising over 640 square miles, which makes it the largest Air Force Base in the free world. Eglin is a military friendly area and also a major tourist attraction due the white-sand beaches.

Glen's transfer was approved, and he was assigned to the Army Paratrooper 6th Ranger Training Battalion. He also served in the Waterborne Operations Section of the Army Ranger School, which trains elite soldiers at Eglin Air Force Base.

Ezekiel 37:1 states, "The hand of the Lord was on me, and brought me out by the spirit of the Lord and set me in the middle of the valley."

The Bible is filled with stories of people who lived their lives under the influence of God. So many blessings come from this scripture. For example, the "hand of the Lord" symbolizes His protective cover over us, in other words, our military.

Despite the sometime pacifist assumptions placed upon Christian belief, many biblical men of God old and renowned have been soldiers and still been faithful men of God. Nowhere was their military service questioned.

Abraham, whom God selected to bless as the Father of His chosen nation, was one of the earliest generals (Gen. 14:14).

Moses and Joshua both led the Israelites in countless battles. David not only fought in wars but also participated in some of the most brutal acts of slaughter recorded in the Bible (2 Sam. 8)

Ultimately, power and authority comes from God, as all things do. I finished my eight-year term with the Young Men's Christian Association (YMCA) in New Orleans, Louisiana. My title was the West Bank associate branch director. We resided on a very nice campus. My neighbors were the New Orleans police department and the United States Marine Reserve headquarters.

Just like in Florida, my biggest supporters were the sheriff department and the military.

One day the New Orleans (NOPD) chief police officer called me and asked if I would participate in a crime prevention walk. Of course, I agreed.

The walk was an iconic group, consisting of the major, police chief, a senator, council members, the Marine commander, and the local news channel to name few.

Our mission was to go door-to-door in one of the most violent, crime-infested, drug-infested communities to hand out pencil, paper, and coloring material to the children.

All policeman and city officials wore bulletproof vest, and I wore my YMCA T-shirt. LOL. Nevertheless, we prayed and started our march.

One of the councilmen led the march and took us to a local nearby community where she once lived. As we walked, she would point out certain homes and gave us the history of it. Her broadcast was sad and shocking because most of the homes were drug infested, and even worse, the children showed signs of neglect and abuse.

The children really embraced us as we gave out our treats, but some of the parents displayed anger and shame because of our presents.

My heart wept for the children because they were surely prisoners in their own homes!

The Shepherd uses his mighty staff to care for and protect the sheep! Meaning, God grants us power to serve and to be merciful.

The military, policeman, parents, or whoever is in a leadership role should move people forward, not condemn or enslave them.

The mightiest power ever unleashed on this earth was not the powerful nuclear bombs dropped on Japan, not even powerful earthquakes or hurricanes. The mightiest power ever unleashed on this earth was when God raised Jesus Christ from the dead!

After serving in the military four years, Glen separated from the Army while he was at Eglin Air Force Base. His priorities at this point in his life were to continue his ministry and be a great father to his daughter.

I was at work one day, and I received a call from a gentleman inquiring about hiring me as his personal trainer. I agreed and told him that I would set up a consultation to see what his goals were.

Upon talking to him, he told me that he wanted to lose fifteen pounds for an upcoming wedding and just wanted to be healthier. Going through my questionnaire, I asked him to tell me about his eating habits. He told me that he loved fried chicken, ice cream, cookies, and sodas—all the bad stuff!

I told him that I could help him achieve his goals, but he would have to modify his eating habits. Boastfully, he informed me that giving up his chicken and ice cream was totally out of the question.

Therefore, I had to decline his request. He wanted to get in shape, but he didn't want to make any personal sacrifices. This is how it is when we attempt to follow Jesus.

In Luke 9:23 Jesus makes it clear when He says, "Whoever wants to be a disciple must deny themselves and take up their cross and follow me." Jesus didn't even have a home. He was homeless, walking from town to town. The cross was a symbol of certain death!

When God asked Glen to follow Him, he knew what was at stake. Glen denied himself by giving up millions of dollars, sacrificed his life by serving in the military, and spent countless hours going town to town preaching God's living word.

We talk a lot about being a Christian means believing in Christ, but we don't talk much about sacrificing and denying ourselves.

One day Glen and I were talking, and he said, "Dad, we're going to set the tone for the Coffee family and generations to come by making things right. And we're going to do it by loving Christ first!"

If one is going to make something right, that means something is wrong.

It's crystal clear to me now, but for the longest time I couldn't understand how a person could love God more than their parents. I have a very good verse to answer that question, but first I want to clarify some things.

Well, first, God gave our parents life. Then he gave us life! Thank You, God! God forbid, but what if you're parents aren't believers and they don't tell you the real story of life? Don't think for one moment that children can't sanctify their parents.

What an awesome topic: children sanctifying their parents! This takes me back to a situation the surfaced during one of my youth basketball seasons at the YMCA. The season was going great, all my teams were full, but one of my seven-to-eight coed teams didn't have a coach.

Ideally, one of the fathers or mothers would volunteer to coach their child and nine other kids. I stepped in and coached the first game to show the parents it was a very simple process. We all took a knee and prayed before the game. All the kids played, and everyone had tremendous fun.

After the game, I told the parents that the blessing was spending quality time with your child! "It's not about winning or losing." Finally, one father stood up and said, "I'll coach the team, Mr. Coffee." After I gladly made the official announcement that the team had a coach, he pulled me to the side and cautiously said, "I'll coach, but there's one problem. I'm an atheist, and we don't pray, and we don't believe in God." The coach's name was Mr. Bee and his son's name was Tad. I said, "That's not a problem, sir, I'll provide all of the training material to make you a great coach, and I'll pray before all games for you."

Everything was going so well. About half way through the season, Coach Bee came into my office unannounced and said, "Mr. Coffee, I'm going to have to give up coaching and pull Tad! I know Tad loves the game and interacting with the other kids, but he keeps asking me about God and Jesus! I just don't have the answers, and it's not going to work for us!"

I pleaded with him and told him that we could study the Bible together or he could be a guest at my church. He declined my offer and insisted that stepping down from coaching would be the best thing.

The next day I made an announcement to Coach Bee's team that he could no longer coach due to personal reasons. Fortunately, one of the fathers did step up to coach the remaining games.

We ended that basketball season on a very good note. The players and parents really enjoyed themselves.

My next sport season was baseball/T-ball. One day I was sorting through my registration forms and surprisingly, I noticed a form from Coach Bee! He had registered his son Tad for baseball and volunteered to coach! He even provided a $250 sponsorship fee to sponsor his team!

I eagerly wanted to talk to him to hear what had changed his heart.

During our baseball coach's meeting, we did have a chance to have a personal one-on-one conversation. Coach Bee shared with me that Tad was devastated when he pulled him out of basketball. And that Tad had been drilling him day and night about coming back to the Y.

The blessing for me came when Coach Bee said that Tad really loved praying to Jesus! He ended our conversation on a very high note, by saying, "You know, Mr. Coffee, maybe someday my family and I will come to know Jesus as you do!" WOW, what a blessing! Praise God!

What God showed us in this story is that sometimes He will go undercover and touch a child's heart in order to open the hearts of their parents!

This is my verse for you: John 3:16 states, "For God so loved the world that He gave His one and only Son, that whoever believes in Him shall not perish but have eternal life." Please underline this next statement. In other words, what God is saying in John 3:16 is, your ears and eyes can't open wide enough for you to see or hear how much I love you! If I become flesh and walk hand-in-hand with you or if I sacrifice My Son maybe, hopefully, that will get your attention!

God's love is the truth, unconditional, flawless, never takes a day off, and, last but not least, it's forever and ever and ever! The problem with our love is that it's some timing. Meaning, if we don't get a call on our birthday or if someone doesn't like our dress or shoes, then that's a major issue.

No matter where you are or where you've been or what you've done, God still loves you!

The question that we should be asking ourselves is, Does God really need anything from us?

In Matthew 19 a rich young ruler approached Jesus and asked Him, "What good things must I do to earn eternal life?" The rich young ruler thought that his popularity and riches made him a prime candidate to enter heaven. And that Jesus would beg him to join His team. Jesus answers his question by saying, "Sell all your possessions and give to the poor, and you will have treasure in heaven. Then come follow me." When the young man heard this, he went away sad because he had great wealth. Money is not the issue here. Of course, we need money. It's the lust of money which is sinful. Jesus knew the young ruler had money, but He also knew the money had him and that he worshipped and idolized it!

God just don't want us loving anything more than Him. When we tithe, that shows God that money doesn't control us. It also makes Him so happy when we freely give, then He just blesses us even more.

God brings true balance in our lives. Earlier in my text, I had mentioned that I grew up in a single-parent home. My mom raised me and my five brothers alone. My father passed when I was very young.

My mother was an excellent provider and multitalented in various ways. She single-handedly encouraged and taught us how to become great fisherman and hunters. Occasionally, she would help me perform small maintenance on my car.

We didn't attend church much, but I'm very thankful that we had a praying mother! She did a great job in showing us the importance of having a relationship with Christ.

I left home when I graduated from high school with a sense of accomplishment and contentment.

Although my mom raised me to be a man, she couldn't teach me how to be a man. She simply couldn't give me what she didn't have.

When I got to college, things were cool. But I started feeling empty, a void, something was missing. I called my younger brother Kendy, and he was experiencing the same thing— emptiness.

We had listened to our relative's philosophies about manhood, but their version was 90 percent worldly and didn't really line up with God's word. There's an old African proverb that says, "It takes a village to raise a child." The widespread use of this proverb by cultures around the world shows its immense relevancy. It's great that everyone understands that children are a blessing from God and we should give a helping hand.

However, when we stay in our village, we all speak the same language, we laugh at the same jokes, and we all dress the same. This concept gives us a false sense of our diverse world! When God takes us out of our comfort zone, our village, the world will judge us into our godly purpose!

The mother eagle will purposely disrupt the nest, making it uncomfortable for the eaglets on a daily basis, showing them that its time. When the young eaglets finally leave and have to provide for themselves. Only then do they discover their true purpose in life! If you're ever going to soar with the eagles and find true manhood, you have to leave the nest. So, after leaving home, the Holy Spirit led my brother and me to the Bible.

We were truly empowered when we read Genesis 1:26. It reads: "Then God said, 'Let us make man in our image, after our likeness.

And let them have dominion over the fish of the sea and over the livestock and over all the earth and over every creeping thing that creeps on the earth!'" WOW.

What God is saying in Genesis is that, not only should we be leaders in our communities, He's also telling us that we men are bred to lead throughout the whole world. Hebrew 10:9 tells us, "A true man, like Jesus, is obedient to the Father's will and is about His Father's business!"

This is good word. As men, we need to pray for understanding because once again we are responsible for the next generation. I assume that every father wants their children to have a better life than they had.

It's vital that a man understands godly manhood before he attempts fatherhood.

Watching Glen raise his daughter is so surreal and such a blessing. My granddaughter will have everlasting blessings because of Glen's faithful service. At this moment in my life, I don't go to many football games anymore or read about Glen jumping from planes. My thrill now is when he calls me to watch my beautiful granddaughter. And that's fine with me.

Without a doubt, he's an awesome soldier for Christ and I know God will have another mission for him soon enough!

Please continue to pray for Glen and me, and we'll do the same for you. And always remember, there's more to life than the pursuit of money!

Epilogue

Glory be to God. In His glory we are glorified. Not only glorified but healed. Not only healed but saved. What is it that you want in life? If you have trouble answering this question directly, that is perfectly fine. Search after Christ and all else will be revealed. Matthew 6:33. If you can easily answer what it is that you want in life, then let me humbly give you pause. We have an idea of happiness, an idea of success, and an idea of fulfillment. Instead of an idea, wouldn't you want to be 100 percent sure? Maybe have a diagram or blueprint of how, who, why, what, when, and where? Can I say only God knows this exactly? Well I am, only He knows. Proverbs 16:1-3.

This approach to life is of course easier said than done. It goes without saying that I, for one, could benefit greatly from following my own advice. I'm trying though, and slowly but surely learning to trust in Him. Although I must admit, I've noticed that after every fall, it isn't myself that gets up. Rather it's Jesus who picks me up. He'll pick me and say, "Yeah, you messed up pretty big … but guess what? I'm here for in times like these. I'm here for you when you need me and here for you when you think you don't." My weakness is His strength, my strength is His love. As in lifting weights, pain is gain. The same is applicable to my life. In pain, I've gained the most. I can only pray the same can be said for the pain that I've caused others.

For those who know me and for those who don't, I ask two things. First, for your sake more than mine, try not to judge me. Pray for me as I hope you pray for yourself. Second, the greatest gift you can give someone is yourself. Jesus gave us himself, His whole self. A stranger is only a stranger out of ignorance. Education is key. For the church to be effective, we must give ourselves. The good, bad, ugly, and indifferent. Give it all. We were created for relationship. Relationship with our Lord and relationship with each other. How can we expect a non-believer to hear what we have to say, if we give only the least of ourselves (our goodness)? Not all of us love Jesus; we all, however, sin. We are all sinners.

For those of us who love and those who don't, let's relate. Love is a hard thing to accomplish without the acknowledgment of a relationship. So whether your neighbor is a "stranger" in line at a coffee shop or a person you see every day, if given the opportunity, share something. We are called to share. Share a head nod, smile, hug, story or testimony. And if they aren't willing to share the moment back, give it to them. Regardless if they receive it or not, God will handle the rest. Whatever your name is, my dad and I both love you. Luke 10:25-37

Glen Coffee Jr.

Endorsements

It is with great pleasure that I endorse Glen Coffee's book. As a Christian, I found this book to be a wonderful account of how a young man walks with Christ and lives out his faith, even when the decisions are difficult. As a career military officer, I very much appreciate Glen's willingness to walk away from professional football in order to serve and defend out freedoms.

—General Buster Ellis, 2-star retired Air Force General

Having known Glen Coffee Sr. and Glen Coffee Jr. for many years I can attest to their strong values and relationship with God. They are patriots having served in our nations great military. I commend them on this book and the message it shares.

— Retired Army Colonel Michael Appe

"Glen Sr. and Glen Jr. are warriors for God and have written a book by sharing their testimonies of how to face any crisis in life including the many challenges we face every day to include making decisions about financial situations that we encounter throughout our lives. The Coffee's share the best approach to solve any decision – a "how to" book for fathers, mothers, and families trying to overcome life's challenges every day."

— Retired Air Force Colonel Rocky Kimpel

About the Author

Glen Sr. Bio

Glen Coffee Sr. was born in New Madrid, Mo., and graduated from Lilbourn High School. He is an inspirational author, veteran, engineer, public speaker and fitness guru who loves to use his passion for practical wisdom to encourage others in reaching their fullest potential. Through his uplifting, unbiased messages, Glen inspires people to discover their true identity in Christ! He served 8 years in the United States Air Force and was also a member of the Air Force boxing team in Madrid Spain. Glen Sr. is also a graduate of Bailey Tech. ITT St. Louis, Mo.; Sikeston Career & Technology Center, Sikeston, Mo.; and the Missouri Welding Institution Nevada, Mo.

Glen Sr.'s professional experience includes 10 years working as an engineer for Boeing Aerospace worldwide. He also served 5 years as the Associate Branch/Sports Director at the Fort Walton Family and 3 years at the West Bank YMCA in New Orleans, LA. Presently Glen Sr. is an Industrial Contractor and works worldwide.

Glen is also the proud father of four adult children and the grandfather of two beautiful granddaughters.

Glen Jr. Bio

Glen Coffee Jr. was born at Eglin Air Force Base, FL. After living in Saudi Arabia from ages 4-10, he attended Bruner Middle School during his adolescence and graduated from Fort Walton Beach, FL. High School in May 2005.

After earning a student-athlete scholarship with the University of Alabama, he became one of the greatest players in Alabama Football history.

All-star running back Glen Coffee compiled 2,107 rushing yards with 14 touchdowns and 5.1 yards per carry.

During Glen's junior year he led the Crimson Tide to a 12-0 undefeated regular season. Due to his record-breaking 2008 season, Glen was named to the ALL-SEC First Team and the Coaches ALL-SEC Second Team. Also, the team's "Most Valuable Player.

Glen entered the NFL Draft in 2009 and was drafted by the San Francisco 49ers in the third round. Due to a Spiritual Calling, he faithfully retired from the NFL after playing only one season.

He was featured on the cover of the world-renowned Sports Illustrated in 2008 and was also a guest on the "700 Club" in 2010.

Glen joined the United States Army in June of 2013 where he spent 4 years serving his country as an elite Army Ranger.

Today, Glen Jr. is a successful author, and assistance coach on legendary Coach Nick Saban's coaching staff at the University of Alabama. He holds a BS in Human Environmental Science, and is a sought-after motivational speaker for the team.

He is also the proud father of Ava Coffee, his beautiful daughter.